PARISH

✳

HADLEY

PARISH

HADLEY

SIXTY YEARS OF AMERICAN DESIGN

SISTER PARISH, ALBERT HADLEY, AND CHRISTOPHER PETKANAS

LITTLE, BROWN AND COMPANY

BOSTON   NEW YORK   TORONTO   LONDON

First Edition

Library of Congress Cataloging-in-Publication Data

   Parish-Hadley : sixty years of American design / Christopher
Petkanas. — 1st ed.
          p.   cm.
   Includes bibliographical references and index.
   ISBN 0-316-70032-0
   1. Parish-Hadley Associates.   2. Interior decoration—United
States—History—20th century.   I. Title.
NK2004.3.P37P48   1995
747.213—dc20   95-946

10 9 8 7 6 5 4 3 2 1

DESIGNED BY DANIA MARTINEZ DAVEY

NIL

Published simultaneously in Canada by Little, Brown & Company (Canada) Limited

Printed in Italy

THIS BOOK IS DEDICATED TO SISTER PARISH

1910–1994

— PARISH-HADLEY ASSOCIATES

acknowledgments

Like decorating a house, writing a book has proven to be the result of passionate collaboration. The following are notable among many who have been invaluable to this project.

Ray Roberts, who first brought us together with Little, Brown and Company; Fredi Friedman, who took up the project and continued to support it through completion. Deborah Geltman and Gayle Benderoff, who provided more than professional advice. Irene Carter, who ushered this project through its many stages with good will and humor, and coordinated an insurmountable inventory of Parish-Hadley archives and photographs into a coherent whole. David Kleinberg, for being liaison to the many parties involved without losing sight of our goals. Betty Ann Hadley, Apple Bartlett, and D. B. Riley for remembering their families' histories and having the pictures to prove it. Dania Martinez Davey, for her elegant and unerring design sense and heroic efforts. Ellen Horan, for determined pursuit of photographs and permissions. S. I. Newhouse and Nancy Novogrod, for support past and present. Also of invaluable help were Diana Edkins, Cynthia Cathcart, and Carole Sheehan. Our heartfelt thanks most sincerely to the many talented and dedicated people who have worked with us in the past and present, and to our clients, who have allowed us the many opportunities to realize our fantasies together.

— **PARISH-HADLEY ASSOCIATES**

Every author hopes to be surrounded by people unselfish enough to make his problem theirs. I was lucky to have friends, family, and colleagues who made the book process easier for me.

In Paris, I am deeply indebted to my friend Nadine Frey, and in New York to Emelie Tolley.

I would also like to thank my father, Ernest (Tasi) Petkanas; Peter Dobbin and Patti O'Brien, for their help with working visits to New York; Nancy Novogrod, my editor at *Travel & Leisure*, for her support and encouragement; Helen Pratt, for advising me professionally; Lisa Frey, for her legal advice; Patricia McColl, for opening up her library; Devon Fredericks; and Mary Hyman and Philip Hyman.

At the *International Herald Tribune* in Paris, I would like to thank Katherine Knorr, John Vinocur, and Mary Mills.

At Parish-Hadley, Irene Carter, David McMahon, Kim Cruise, Nancy Porter, Libby Cameron, and Beth Martell were all helpful.

Finally, I have Mrs. Parish to thank for such a rich and worthy subject.

— **CHRISTOPHER PETKANAS**

contents

foreword

My first encounter with Mrs. Parish, known to the world as Sister, was unfortunate — at least for her. It took place over forty years ago. Mrs. Parish had been summoned to my parents' house in New Jersey to make some improvements and was waiting for my mother in the living room. Her ears were suddenly assailed by an unholy clatter and some of the worst language she said she had ever heard. It was me, aged ten, riding my horse up the steps into the front hall for a reason I have now forgotten, and having a fight with Clark, the outraged butler, who was trying, unsuccessfully, to keep us out.

Horrified though she was, Mrs. Parish and I have been friends — great friends — ever since. Throughout our long rapport I have had the pleasure of watching her work her magic on a series of houses and apartments belonging to friends and to four generations of my family. What always amazes me is her versatility. Mrs. Parish managed to exorcise the gloom of my grandmother's Rhenish castle in Bernardsville as successfully as she helped to create a delightful one-room apartment for my daughter, Beatrice, using mostly things from Walter's Wonderful World of Wicker! Time and again she has transformed disparate assortments of furniture and objects into wonderfully coherent rooms. The look is festive, life-enhancing, but never the least bit showy or "decorated." The air of fastidiousness and patrician coziness is evoked by Mrs. Parish better than anybody else and it always redounds to the owner's credit.

Like her, Albert Hadley is a joy to work with. In my experience he and Mrs. Parish have an ideal partnership. Whereas her approach can perhaps best be described as Anglo-American, with a huge sense of her own family's influence, Albert Hadley is pure American: a meticulous designer with impeccable pared-down taste. He has a modern architect's feeling for space and grace and is always ready to experiment. The more contemporary Hadley qualities complement the more traditional Parish ones to perfection. They both know exactly how their clients wish to live and get the point immediately — in my book that's coming up trumps!

— ANNETTE DE LA RENTA
CASA DE MADERA
DOMINICAN REPUBLIC
FEBRUARY 1995

Parish-Hadley Associates

IN NOVEMBER 1962, NOT KNOWING QUITE WHAT TO EXPECT, Albert Hadley stood on the mat in front of apartment number eleven at 39 East 79th Street. He wore a gray flannel suit from Brooks Brothers, a blue shirt, and a black knit tie. He looked owlish, donnish, completely un-frivolous, which is very much the way he looks today. He rang the buzzer. It was five-thirty.

The native Tennesseean had a glancing acquaintance with the woman who answered the door, a woman with a kind of preemptive Edwardian aura and an entry in the Social Register to match. She was Mrs. Henry Parish II, a figure known to her circle by the curious family nickname "Sister." As someone steeped in the wide history and culture of decoration, Albert Hadley certainly knew everything there was to know about her life and work — how she had bucked the caste system by setting herself up in business during the depression in Far Hills, New Jersey; the houses she had done for glamorous A-list clients like

Albert and Sister in the doorway of their office at 22 East 69th Street.

Mrs. Vincent Astor and the Charles W. Engelhards, who also happened to be friends with whom she regularly stayed the weekend; the fact that at this moment she was hard at work with Mrs. Kennedy on the White House.

Albert himself had grown up in and around Nashville in comfortable though by no means luxurious surroundings. "You could definitely not say that my parents' life was one of great ease." As a boy he was captivated by everything to do with domestic life, from the stage on which it is played out to its form and logic. The fact that the driveway of the family house brought you to the back rather than the front door exasperated him unreasonably. "Change it," the precocious youngster threatened his father, a dealer in buggies and farm implements, "or I'll run away."

Albert later studied art and design at Peabody College, then trained with the local decorator A. Herbert Rodgers, the best in the South when Albert was coming of age. Mr. Rodgers impressed him with his French-inflected house (mansard roof, parquet de Versailles), and with Chippendale chairs whose crackled white leather was held down with antique silver nails. He also introduced him to the possibilities of silver-leaf Chinese tea paper as a wall covering. That introduction had resonance.

The meeting between Mrs. Parish and Albert Hadley came out of a party she attended the night before. Over dessert she asked her dinner partner, Tiffany design director Van Day Truex, if by any chance he knew of "some young man" who could give her a hand, absorb some of the responsibility at the office. Mr. Truex suggested she see his friend Albert Hadley, whom he had once regarded as his protégé and who had attended and taught at the Parsons School of Design. He was now with McMillen and rising fast.

Greeting him in stocking feet, standing in the antique-mirrored hall Eloi Bordelon had painted over with an ornamental network of bamboo, Mrs. Parish asked her forty-two-year-old visitor to "Zip me up, will you?" Exactly ten years her junior, slightly disarmed, he did what she wanted. Manners are everything to Mrs. Parish, and right away she liked the Southern, deferential, unforced ones displayed by her guest. Then she asked if he wouldn't mind being barman.

"After that we talked well into the night," Albert recalls today. "We've been talking ever since."

Mrs. Parish later told decorative painter Richard Lowell Neas, to whom she assigned the treillage pool house at Greentree, the legendary Whitney estate on Long Island: "Meeting Albert saved my life."

Sister Parish and Albert Hadley went on to form the most exciting, influential, and talked-about American decorating firm of the second half of the twentieth century. Binding them from the start has been a high-pitched appreciation of luxury, quality, comfort, glamour, and romance. A mutual love of handcrafts and quirky, exotic furniture also destined them for each other. One thinks of the dwarf Louis XVI tables that filled Mrs. Parish's former office on East 69th Street. Or of the painted and gilded Portuguese console with cabriole legs mimicking human limbs in high-topped shoes that has trailed Albert from house to house since the 1960s.

If their first rencontre sounds apocryphal, too novelistic to be true, both principals swear to it on the heads of their grandchildren and godchildren. And they do not gloss over the more difficult aspects of their collaboration, chinks that have earned them the title of the Odd Couple of American decorating.

"Of course we have our differences," says Albert, "and they can be enormous."

"We fight a lot, but we have complemented each other," says Sister. "It's been an interesting balance."

While she is known for her firm attachment to, in the best sense, everything old-fashioned, Albert is perhaps best described as a modernist with a bad case of nostalgia. The peculiar, mutually stimulating tension arising from these differences and their shared point of view has produced some of the most important rooms of the last three decades. Mrs. Parish had done fine on her own, and Albert Hadley would have surely left McMillen and soloed successfully, carrying the baton passed to him by Billy

Baldwin. But there is no doubt that the oeuvre Mrs. Parish and Albert Hadley created jointly could never have been created by either of them alone.

"I've always thought that either of them was better than anyone," says Boston-based Bill Hodgins, who started at the firm as a junior assistant in 1964. "But together!"

The living room Mrs. Parish and Albert created for the 1978 Kips Bay Show House in New York is a perfect example of how their creative partnership has operated. It started out as his job — a summer scheme for a fictitional collector of modern art who also happened to own an assortment of very traditional upholstered furniture. The walls were painted a no-color gray. From the ceiling tinted shell pink hung an important Waterford chandelier that centered the room. A bright, crisp, red-and-white-striped cotton was specially designed for the chairs' and stool's deliberately loose slipcovers (dustcovers, actually), simple straight-hanging curtains, and shirred Venetian-style valances. The floor was practically bare, and an oval mirror in a gilt frame hung over the fireplace.

Then, just as the paintings and drawings and sculpture started coming in, Mrs. Parish came by for a look. "Oh, I can fix this," she said. Albert agreed she could make her additions: vibrant red roller shades under the curtains, an extraordinary English needlework rug, flower pictures, photographs, even her own straw hat.

"Sis went out shopping to Garrick Stephenson's and came back with all this ravishing romantic stuff — little novel tables, candlesticks," remembers Albert. "She just sort of threw it all around and made her magic. She accessorized the room and made it cozy and feminine. My concept had been entirely different. But I have to concede that what she added was sensational."

A similar thing happened in the Manhattan living room of Enid Annenberg Haupt, the great horticulturist for whom the company has done some of its best work. "I would have covered the seating in burlap and left it at that," recalls Albert, "but Sis wanted Floral Bouquet and Border, the glazed chintz she is always associated with, and brocade for the incidental pieces. Left on her own, she probably would have gone with a more definite color for the walls, but I had decided on a pale peachy beige. And she would have had more furniture and a more relaxed furniture plan. In general the whole thing would have been more sensual. But we were working together. Each of us contributed to the mix."

Together and individually Mrs. Parish and Albert Hadley have worked on landmark houses and apartments for the Edgar Bronfmans, the William S. Paleys, Annette de la Renta when she was married to Samuel Reed, Carter Burden, Mrs. Thomas Jefferson Coolidge, Connie Mellon, Gordon and Ann Getty, Happy Rockefeller, Al and Tipper Gore, and Freddy and Louise Melhado, who has gone on with the firm as Mrs. Henry Grunwald. With Albert Hadley at her elbow to give her strength and their increasing popularity to give her courage, Mrs. Parish was able to confront Eleanor Brown of McMillen when her old rival would tweak her in the elevator of the D&D Building. From behind the veil of a rabbit-eared hat and in a tiny voice to match, Mrs. Brown would ask, "Still in business, Sister?"

"Of course I am," Mrs. Parish would respond coolly.

Sister and Albert's teaming up — they became partners in 1964 — has also produced a catalogue of signature "innovations." Wildly painted and stained floors, patchwork quilts, four-poster beds, rag rugs, painted valances, handwoven bedspreads, and knitted throws are the ones most often cited, but there are also needlework of every description, botanical prints and porcelain, hooked "zebra" rugs, architectural use of mirror, the silver-leaf tea paper in which A. Herbert Rogers schooled Albert, upholstery that is more voluptuous than any of the competition's, sumptuously festooned curtains with pleated ribbon trim and contrast linings in small patterns, whimsically decorative and elaborate surface finishes (one thinks of aubergine walls sanded and varnished to a reflective sheen),

Working together in Albert's office.

sheen), and baskets as cachepots poised everywhere from the bench on the back porch in Maine to the Queen Anne end table in the drawing room on Park Avenue.

"Of course," says Nancy Novogrod, *House & Garden*'s last editor, from 1988 to 1993, "Sister was the first significant champion of using American crafts in decorating."

Because the company has always functioned as a sort of exclusive graduate school servicing the upper reaches of the decorating industry, the "innovations" have seen wide, wide diffusion. In addition to Bill Hodgins. alumni include Mark Hampton, David Easton, Keith Irvine, Robert Moore, Kevin McNamara, Bunny Williams, Harold Simmons, Mariette Himes Gomez, Tice Alexander, Nicholas Miles Pentecost, Brian McCarthy, John Cronin, and Robert Yoh. One of the most important talents ever em-

ployed by the firm was Gary Hager, who died in 1991. David Kleinberg, Libby Cameron, Brian Murphy, and Pamela Banker are on staff today, and David McMahon heads the design department.

"Every promising young decorator I know has learned a thing or two (or hundred) from this unlikely — and likable — pair," says Marian McEvoy, editor in chief of *Elle Decor*. "Sister and Albert are not about tricky or groovy trends."

Mario Buatta's look depends so much on his friend Sister's, he'd be the first to admit that if it weren't for her, he'd be out of work. But David Easton worries about over-enthusiastic disciples. "Mrs. Parish's intelligent WASP reserve tells her that curtains can be an inch too long so they bunch nicely on the floor, but not more than an inch."

The iron credo she forged with Albert takes for granted that a room must be at once comfortable, practical, outside of fashion, and appropriate — no tin palm trees in the country dining room, no muslin curtains in the one in town. (Caution: all rules are made to be broken.) Of course a room must also be beautiful, a word that is understood to embrace chic. When one of the above is sacrificed to another, Parish-Hadley Associates, Inc., as the twenty-five-strong company has been known since 1982, is aware it risks losing its edge.

"The thing that is most reassuring is that what they do now is exactly what they did when I was an assistant in 1964," says Edward Lee Cave. "Their taste is perpetual." In the 1970s Billy Baldwin told Valentine Lawford: "Through all the years, Sister has done — and still does — by far the most attractive, seductive, luxurious bedrooms of any decorator in America." He was referring to the sensuous shapes of her furniture, the intriguing mixture of textures (a worn cotton quilt against the finest linens), silk-and-mohair throws dyed to match the room and threaded with satin ribbons.

Such interiors affirm the Old World Wharton-esque values that were Mrs. Parish's nursery formula: family, continuity, permanence. ("My dreams have always been about the kind of life that Sis represents," says Albert.)

Creating a look of continuity for others can be a brutal process. Ask any who have been "tea-carted" or "trayed," terms that describe Mrs. Parish's practice, at the start of a job, of cleansing rooms of their gewgaws (usually a lot of coy wedding presents) by wheeling through a tea cart or carrying through a tray and piling on the offenders. When a client asked Albert to cast his eye around her apartment the afternoon before an important dinner party just to ensure everything was in order, the woman came home to find all the beloved trinkets she'd added since he'd decorated the place banished. "I've been trayed!" she screeched. "Trayed!!"

"When I first went to see Albert some twenty years ago about my town house, he said he couldn't undertake any job without Sister's approval," remembers Glenn Bernbaum, the owner of Morti-

mer's, the Manhattan restaurant popular with the sort of people for whom Parish-Hadley decorate. "She had to approve the client as much as the job in those days. Since then we've become friends. But she still has that withering way of casting her eye around a room at a party and saying, 'Who *are* all these people?'"

Pomposity and gratuitous opulence, no matter how good the furniture filling a Parish-Hadley job, are outlawed. "She thinks it's bad manners for a room to look pretentious," says Mark Hampton, who fairly worships Mrs. Parish. "No house, however grand, is ever stiff, formal, or forbidding," says Harold Simmons, who ran the design department for many years. "The company's point of view is that great furniture is for use. There's always a place to put your drink and a lamp to read by. Parish-Hadley rooms are not museum rooms."

Mrs. Parish's anglophilia, the chief expression of which is her great fondness for flowered chintz, gets the "old" message across instantly. When, in *House & Garden*, Georgina Howell asked Mrs. Parish if she was "happy for her style to be summed up as 'cabbage roses and Aubusson,'" she shot back, "It's always been my cup of tea. Of course, I've been copied a lot."

"My first influence was Sibyl Colefax," Mrs. Parish told Patrick O'Higgins in 1979, referring to the co-founder, in 1938, of the London firm Colefax & Fowler. "I learned the extraordinary art of understated British comfort from her. [All those] luscious, mouth-watering glazed chintzes. . . . I spread her gospel and then added a few footnotes." Later, Lady Colefax's partner, John Fowler, and his partner, the Virginia-born Nancy Lancaster, were also shaping influences. Both Mrs. Parish and Albert Hadley responded to an element of off-the-cuff unconventionality in their work, of oddball personal expression that took everything down a peg. Overwhelming evidence that Colefax & Fowler rooms hadn't been "done" yesterday, or even ten years ago, but over decades by successive generations of the same family, also charmed them.

"It's that look that, no matter how much you've

Mrs. Parish's charming canopy bed in the 79th Street
apartment.

spent, if it looks like you've spent nothing, then
you've won the game, match, set," says Keith Irvine.
"All your great and marvelous possessions are
played down to the point where they almost disap-
pear." Mr. Irvine was working for Colefax & Fowler
but hoping to go to America when John Fowler se-
cured a job for him with Mrs. Parish in 1958. He
later helped establish the textile company Clarence
House before launching his association with Tom
Fleming.

Tom Parr, who heads Colefax & Fowler today,
says that before Nancy Lancaster and Mrs. Parish
came on the scene, "design as such had always been
the most important and perhaps the only aspect of
interior decorating. But these women took an enormous amount of trouble to bring comfort, luxury,
and style to the way people lived. And their posi-
tions in society enabled them to attract clients on
their own level." Mr. Parr adds that just as Mrs.
Lancaster introduced John Fowler to the washed

palette of Palladian villas, and taught him how to
stir together grand furniture with the everyday. "I
am sure Sister Parish must have been a tremendous
help to Albert Hadley. While keeping his original
modern, pared-down approach, he adopted her
standards of luxury and comfort. It's been a marvelous 'marriage.'"

Sister's and Albert's divergent ideals were fully
expressed in the living room he designed for her in
the early 1970s at 960 Fifth Avenue. "By this time
Sis was beginning to feel she wanted to be modern,"
says Albert. "I gave her high-gloss aubergine vinyl
walls, polished aluminum Levelor blinds, a silver
tea-paper ceiling that quickly tarnished to gold,
plaster lamps, an abstract painting by Anthony Tor-
tora, an entire wall of mirror, and billowy unlined
pink taffeta curtains that she really wasn't ready for.
Over the floor — bleached almost white — I put a
dhurrie rug. Modern lighting was another important
element. The expert I called in used quite a lot of
indirect effects, rigging lights in the reveals of the
deeply recessed windows, as well as underneath
console tables to dispel shadows. But the rest was all
Sis — the enveloping sofas, the chaise longue with a
fur throw draped over its end, the masses of soft
downy pillows everywhere."

"It has been suggested that the pairing of Sister
and Albert harks back to that of Nancy Lancaster
and John Fowler," notes Nancy Novogrod, "but I
would invent a far more divergent coupling of design forebears — Jean-Michel Frank, with his daring modernist sensibility, and Mrs. Lancaster, with
her worldly and gracious look. The coming together
of Sister and Albert is almost that surprising, and
yet it works. The Parish-Hadley style bridges the
twentieth century, a completely original distillation
of two unique points of view."

"Sister invented quiet good taste," according to
Richard Lowell Neas. "To me she did it better than
anyone, including Nancy, John, and La Mendl. In
addition she charmed the birds out of the trees.
She had the lowdown on all the girls and kept
them on the edges of their fauteuils listening to

the latest." Writing of Enid Annenberg Haupt, Christopher Hemphill put his finger on the firm's English connection, observing, "[Mrs. Haupt's] ideas about gardening bear the same English influence as Parish-Hadley's ideas about decoration, and complement them, having the same hallmarks: expensive simplicity, a deliberate downplaying of grandeur, and a contrived apparent lack of contrivance."

At the same time it should be noted that Mrs. Parish's love of things English is brilliantly and delicately cut with a natural feeling for the lightness, prettiness, and romance of French eighteenth-century decoration. The oyster, blush pink, and buff gray of the gay rustling dresses worn by the bow-mouthed porcelain figures in Fragonard's *The Pursuit*, combined with the painting's happy soufflé air of uncomplicated femininity, somehow conspire to suggest the drawing room in her Fifth Avenue maisonette today.

If Mrs. Parish has been the most famous decorator in America for almost the last thirty-five years — and she has — her retreat at Dark Harbor on the island of Islesboro, Maine, which she considers nothing less than the center of the universe, has had a lot to do with incising her look on the public consciousness. The nineteenth-century sea captain's Cape with jutting additions is a style bubble of tole roosters, granny afghans, carved wood bunnies, knitting bags sewn to chair arms, fanciful wicker furniture, ragged bits of driftwood painted to look like half-eaten watermelon slices, and decoupage a-go-go. When pictures of the Cape were first published, in *House & Garden* in 1967, Elaine Greene, an editor at the magazine then, says they were the decorating shot heard around the country.

"I remember the pictures coming in and all of us being absolutely astounded," recalls Ms. Greene. "Four patterned chintzes in one room — no one had ever seen anything like that before. And courageous color" — crushed raspberry, imperial yellow, the apple green of a Lily Pulitzer shirtdress — "was combined in a courageous way that only Mrs. Parish

could manage. Most people don't realize it today, but her house on Islesboro is where the whole American country thing first started. Mary Emmerling, Martha Stewart — they all owe it to Sister."

As to Sister's and Albert's differences, their partnership is one that, on paper at least, should never have flown. She has told a thousand reporters a thousand times that she never went to school, knows less than nothing, can't work a tape measure. "If I'm any good at all I have my instincts and the family rooms I grew up in to thank." Even the bookkeepers at the office came to know the story by heart. "No one could really learn from her because she's so natural, so instinctive," says Lillian Leifert, who was head of the accounting department when she retired in 1990 after twenty-five years. "Without schooling she became the queen of decorators."

Albert, by stiff contrast, is a natural teacher. Having taught at the Parsons School of Design for five years, he is accustomed to nurturing. "He was

A corner of Mr. Hadley's bedroom—1965.

always very good about having an assistant — no other decorator would ever give you the latitude, the support," says Brian McCarthy, who started his own business in 1992 after eight years with the company. "From day one he would have you accompany him to every meeting on every job, which is rare. Most people in his position are so insecure they're afraid to let their assistants get too close to the client because they don't want to lose control. But with Albert it's just the opposite. He actually encourages you to develop your own rapport."

It is no secret that Albert's precise Parsons training put him at odds with Mrs. Parish in the first years of their collaboration. Discussing how to treat a library window, she remarked, "Number seven will do perfectly." When he asked what number seven was, she pulled out of her bag a piece of cardboard with a handful of curtain designs on it, indicating the one she felt fit the bill. She found it surprising if not shocking that at McMillen there were no such things as stock designs, that Albert was used to making elaborate muslin mock-ups and to paying good money to a young man who did nothing but scale lampshades!

When the surprise finally wore off she saw the wisdom and utility — and beauty — of his disciplined and careful approach. She also started to perceive the payoffs of his considering a decorating question from an historical or architectural point of view when such consideration was invited. Hence their work began to pack a double wallop: his scrupulous backgrounds, her genius with furniture and accessories. Sister and Albert's very first job together, the Edgar Bronfman apartment on Park Avenue, brought out the best in both of them. Albert tore out walls, moved the staircase, and eliminated moldings. Sister occupied herself with Lowestoft china and the client's exquisite French furniture.

Furniture and its disposition interest Mrs. Parish perhaps most. "She can get more of it into a single room than most decorators get into an entire apartment," says David Kleinberg. "Her criteria for a furniture plan is always, How many people can sit down?" "Her great flair is for arranging furniture,

which I've always thought separated the sheep from the goats," observes Keith Irvine. Mark Hampton: "Mrs. Parish can do a medium-sized drawing room with thirty places to sit, no problem."

Libby Cameron, whose great-uncle was the all-around bon vivant Rory Cameron, says Mrs. Parish always pictures a room filled with people — "Twelve places to sit is okay but obviously sixteen is better. Often you visit a job with her for the first time, the client is there, and she scowls and squints and doesn't say much — 'Wouldn't it be nice if we did this and maybe we should change that.' But then once you leave she becomes more expansive. In the car on the way back into town she might do one of her famous little plans on the back of an envelope — you know, a sofa the size of a dot and a lamp the size of the moon. But you know just what she means, she crams it all in, and it makes perfect sense. It would be a mistake, though, to think she has a secret. It's her eye. She was born with it. Other decorators attempt the same thing and the results are jumbled, overcrowded — disastrous."

If Mrs. Parish's pet cause is creature comfort, Albert Hadley's is "the chic of suitability." "One does not wear a beautiful ball gown to a picnic. By not wearing it you are not denying the quality of the picnic. It is just not suitable. On the other hand, you don't wear a tennis costume to the Court of St. James's.

"Well," he adds, "it's the same with decorating."

Though it is difficult to unravel her real feelings on the subject, Sister always says she wishes she had Albert's scholarship. And yet intellectual decoration, which he loves — Carlos de Beistegui, say, miming baron James de Rothschild — causes her to tune out instantly. Neither is it his partner Albert is addressing when he preaches the virtuous ability of modernism to streamline daily life. Though it is an old joke in the trade that, armed with a bolt of La Portugaise or Floral Bouquet and Border, "Albert can do Sister better than Sister can," his real world is the world of Jean-Michel Frank sycamore bridge tables, Armin Postler nail sculptures, and the scrapbooks of far-ranging visual stimuli he spends hours composing on weekends at his small Italianate Victorian house in Southport, Connecticut. One scrapbook, titled "People," includes pictures of Colette in bed writing, the Duke of Windsor in a windowpane suit standing in front of The Mill outside Paris, Babe Paley in her Syrie Maugham living room at Kiluna, the Rothschilds at Mouton, the Countess of Kenmare (Rory Cameron's mother) at La Fiorentina, young Lord Herbert dressed as a page and clutching a sword, an older Lord Herbert dressed in a suit and clutching a cocktail, the Marquise de Harcourt surrounded by her three great-grandchildren — and Twiggy.

"Albert's interest in Frank made him a natural member of that band of tastemakers that included Van Day Truex and Billy Baldwin," says Louise Grunwald, the model Hadley client. "And like Billy, he doesn't have an ounce of greed. He doesn't give a damn about selling you the $50,000 commode. Maybe he should, but he doesn't. You know he picks things up on the street, don't you? Those of us who've been his friends for years have been known to call the office with bulletins like: 'Madison Avenue between Seventy-third and Seventy-fourth. West side of the street. Sofa. Bye.' Then he sends his trucker to pick it up."

Albert's outlook is made even more intriguing, and complex, by his consuming, flip-side, starry-eyed interest in glamour and fantasy. Any conversation with him on twentieth-century decoration lands on these benchmarks: Diana Vreeland's giddy questions posed in the pages of *Harper's Bazaar* ("Why don't you whitewash a pair of old linen-closet steps and use on a porch for finger bowls and jars full of flowers or as a child's bedside table for lamps, books and pencils?"), Elsie de Wolfe's scalloped Lucite chair with a printed leopard seat, Syrie Maugham's all-white drawing room in the King's Road, Dorothy Draper's confectionery baroque plasterwork for New York's Essex House, Ruby Ross Wood's own swan-post bed, Sibyl Colefax's palm-based plaster tables, William Pahlmann's often outrageous model rooms for Lord & Taylor. One had a couple of chartreuse calfskin rugs thrown over a bleached floor

embedded with mirrored baguettes a few inches from the skirting board: "The Room with the Diamond Necklace." For Albert, all these people were the embodiment of "spirit and wit and style."

Beyond his battle to keep these elements from being bred out of his metier, he and Mrs. Parish, more than any other decorators, dedicate themselves to how a house is run, how the gears move and at what speed. Pulling up for a first site visit in her station wagon, seated next to the driver, Mrs. Parish is known to go right for the mudroom, the second-floor slop closet, and the maid's sitting room. "Where does the staff go to the bathroom?" she wants to know. "How many laundry baskets will we need?" "Where do the brooms go?" "Has anyone thought of hangers?" "The linen closet is too small. What we need is a linen *room*."

In Mrs. Parish's linen rooms, squares of cardboard covered in pretty patterned wallpaper are inserted between napkins and placemats of different color or design, so that if you want to use the pink ones at the bottom of the stack, they can be removed without disturbing the others. Drawers are kept sweet-smelling with lavender sachets from Provence or scented papers from Venice. Perfumed rings from Floris in London are placed atop the lightbulbs in her lamps. Trays with sprigged and scalloped cloths in starched organdy await in the pantry, ready to indulge guests with breakfast in bed. "Don't forget a flower and the morning paper."

One evening in the fall of 1991, over drinks with Albert in her Manhattan library, with its tortoise-shell birdcage, glazed lobster bisque walls, and Queen Anne secretary filled with ivory objects pushed, improbably, right up against the bookcases, the subject inevitably came around to comfort. Mrs, Parish reflected: "I like to think the rooms we do are completely usable, that there's no space that hasn't got a reason. And they're comfortable — everyone's got everything they need. But comfort means different things to different people, I find. Deep downy upholstery is absolutely what I have always been all about. And that birdcage. I couldn't live in this library without that birdcage."

Looking Back

by Sister Parish

EVEN MY AUNT JOAN, HOPELESSLY SENTIMENTAL about every member of our family, admitted that I was a hideous baby. After staring for days at my scrunched-up face and straight brown hair, my father finally pried my eyes open, only to discover that they were dull brown. "We'll always dress her in brown," Mother is reported to have said. "It's our only possible hope."

My birth certificate read Dorothy May Kinnicutt, but the name Sister was hung on me by my three-year-old brother, Frankie. It has not been an easy cross to bear. I often receive calls from religious groups asking me if I'd meet refugees at the dock. And when I was asked to help "do" the White House, a headline announced, "Kennedys Pick Nun to Decorate White House."

The only girl in a family with three boys, I was born by mistake in our house in Morristown, New Jersey. I was supposed to have entered the world properly in our New York house, but Mother and I didn't quite have the time.

The day was July 15, 1910, and my slightly premature arrival was one of the last occasions when the precise, reassuring timetable of our lives would be interrupted for many years to come.

At home with my Pekingese, Yummy, in a 1968 portrait by Aaron Schickler.

Fifteen days later I was aboard the *Bar Harbor Express*, heading toward the first of my eighty-five summers at Dark Harbor on the island of Islesboro, Maine. The windows of the children's stateroom were draped against contamination with linen sheets. I traveled in a white wicker bassinet with pink ribbons, the same bassinet that had carried Mother and her mother, the same bassinet that would carry my daughter and her daughter. I was receiving, quite unconsciously, my first lesson in good things.

At Rockland, Maine, our entourage boarded the *J. T. Moss*, the Eastern Steamship ferry that carried us the short distance to our island. Met at the dock by surreys and buckboards, we traveled around the harbor and through the pine woods to my grandparents' house on the point. Touching the ocean, practically, on three sides, it was built by my grandfather just after a trip to the Tyrol. The house is owned by my brother Gory's family now, and nothing about it has ever changed over the years. From here you can watch the sun set over the Camden Hills, and watch it rise again over the sailing yachts that fill the harbor. Today, on the porch of my own house on the island, I sometimes take it for granted that the clock has stopped.

Nothing around me is without a story. There are a hundred pieces of golden oak, now painted white with enamel, that my husband, Harry, and I bought with the house for one hundred dollars. There is a basket we brought home from Italy, now filled with sweet peas. And there are Mother's chaise piled with fluted linen pillows from the Parish family; my father's mahogany book holder, which folds down to become a tea table, made by Asprey and attached to the arm of his favorite chair with a swinging brass support; a needlework border that takes the place on the mantel of lace that had, sadly, been washed once too often. On the other side of the house, I sleep in the same maple four-poster I was born in.

None of us who grew up there, who knew the coves, the power of the water, the picnics, the little movie house, the only store, the dances in the grand ballroom, will ever forget it. It forms a bond among us. No words have to be spoken.

A sense of continuity is extremely important to me, and it is, I hope, implicit in my decorating. As a child I discovered the happiness that familiar things can bring, simply knowing that when you round the corner, nothing will have changed. That lucky part of my life I try now to instill in each house that I do. Some think a decorator should change a house. I try to give a house permanence.

Expressing personal feelings and memories is the essence of decorating. People who insist on hiding grandmother's worn wicker are to me lacking in a sense of what I call "home." The first thing I ever bought on my own was a cobbler's bench. My pride in that purchase is still with me, and the bench is right there in my barn in Maine. It is a memory, a happy feeling, not a cobbler's bench.

The memory that emerges strongest from my childhood is the strict, comforting pattern of our family life. Played out in four different houses, it went like clockwork. We would leave Dark Harbor for Morristown the day after Labor Day. No questions. We would leave Morristown for the house in New York City the Monday after Thanksgiving. No questions. We would leave New York to return to New Jersey on the Thursday before Good Friday. No questions. We would leave the country for Maine on July 2. No questions. Often, in the spring, we would visit Paris, where we had an apartment at 23 quai d'Orsay. No questions.

Upon returning to New Jersey each fall, our only fear was that school would soon be starting. Every morning Mademoiselle would sponge the Boston waterproof around the soles of our shoes so they'd be black and shiny for school. Mealtimes were sacred, and if you weren't on time, you didn't eat. Bedtime was on the dot.

I'm a great believer in manners, and ours were always correct. When someone was introduced, the boys bowed and I curtsied. No one ever picked up a fork until the first bite was between Mother's lips. These things are all but gone today, and I think it's tragic.

A strong sense of family was instilled in me from the beginning. Our American forebears included Cotton Mather and Oliver Wolcott, who signed the Declaration of Independence, and as children we were told that "a strong wire of character" stretched from them through all the generations of our family. If the wire was strong enough, we understood, anything we might do would turn out right.

Our New York neighborhood for the first six years of my life was Murray Hill, an area that could be roughly defined, socially if not geographically, as being between 34th Street and 38th Street, and between Lexington Avenue and Madison Avenue. In those days it was considered "uptown." The houses were mostly large, comfortable brownstones. It was a rich neighborhood, but with the exception of J. P. Morgan's house, there were few mansions to rival those on Fifth Avenue. Top hats were still common, footmen helped ladies sweep down from their carriages, and children wore English tweeds with velvet collars. Just around the corner were my Kinnicutt grandparents. He was Dr. Francis P. Kinnicutt, one of the foremost physicians in the country. When patients summoned him to their bedside, they often sent their private railway car to ease the trip.

My grandmother Eleanora Kissel Kinnicutt was a woman of distinct character and frozen expression — all bust, bustles, and severity. Her principal charity was placing No Spitting signs in subways. Both she and my grandfather campaigned for the Street Cleaning Department. But no matter what their achievements, the Kinnicutts had appalling taste: polar bear rugs, moose heads, antlers, golden oak furniture, and dreary pastoral paintings.

My maternal grandparents, the Bayard Tuckermans, were much more social. Annie Tuckerman was a pretty woman of enormous charm, the opposite of my grandmother Kinnicutt. People were drawn to her house for the latest gossip. Her delivery was stinging. Mother, who was to inherit her charm and wit, was the object of many of her notable remarks. On one occasion, Grandmother Tuckerman introduced her to President Cleveland

The summer house — Dark Harbor, Maine — seen from the seaside garden.

by saying, "I'm sorry, but today May looks like a piece of tissue paper." Bayard Tuckerman was a gentle, adoring husband who wrote biographies of General Lafayette and Peter Stuyvesant.

My father was G. Herman Kinnicutt. He went to Harvard and, with his uncle, formed the brokerage firm of Kissell, Kinnicutt, which later merged with Kidder, Peabody & Co. My father ran the firm successfully until he died of a heart attack on the day Pearl Harbor was bombed. Like most successful men of his time, he had a dimension beyond the business, sporting, and social lives he led. He was a connoisseur of English and American furniture. My father and I used to bicycle all over New Jersey exploring antiques shops, and whenever we tinkled the bell on a shop door, he would invariably buy me a Staffordshire figure. Thus collections are born.

A background in furniture is essential to decorating, but without taste, all the knowledge in the world won't help you make a room look right. My father had good taste in a scholarly sense. Mother had instinctive good taste. He would find an important eighteenth-century desk. She would know that the charcoal sketch of my brother should go above

13

Pages 14–15: Sister Parish abandoned floral chintz — temporarily — for this scheme in her new apartment in the early 1970s.

Pages 16–17: The return to romanticism.

it, that the crystal candlestick should go on it, that this figurine and that Chinese bowl would balance the family photographs that brought the desk to life.

"Everything in its place" was almost an obsession with Mother. When she came home from the hospital just before she died, she had the orderlies carry her on a stretcher from room to room. Wherever she went she found something an inch out of place and put it back.

The first room I can recall was my family's sitting room in Morristown. The walls were white, the floor covered with yellow matting and a needlework rug of roses. The furniture was wicker painted white, upright and stiff. Some of the tables were covered in lace to the floor, and the chairs had hard buttoned cushions. The cushions, curtains, and window-seat pad, its ruffle fluted and starched, were of cotton printed with vines and roses that looked like the flowers in Mother's bowls. The wood basket with a hoop handle was always full.

Family pictures in silver frames were everywhere, while on the mantel, which had a deep organdy and lace ruffle, was a gold clock with two heavy columns under a glass dome. On each side of the clock were candlesticks with angels clustered at their bases. And there was a silver bell. To this day I can hear it summoning someone.

The lampshades were the room's feature — paper cut out by my father in the form of lacy flowers above bases of twisted glass. I remember Mother saying, "Please put a wash of pale pink inside them." Years later, in Paris, I heard those same words when Madame Ritz conducted me on a tour of the Hôtel Ritz. She said, "In doing a room, you have only one rule to remember: Always line your lampshades with pale pink." The light was meant to be flattering to one's complexion.

White wicker crept back into my life when I was nineteen and decorating my own first house, in New Jersey. And today my house in Maine feels like home because it looks like the first room that I remember.

In Mother's day decorators were not in evidence. People did their own houses, enlisting if needed upholstery shops like Lenygon & Morant, Mrs. Hooper, or French & Co. When my parents moved the family from East 36th Street to 65 East 82nd Street, it was Schmitt & Co. they hired. Here was change indeed! A six-story town house with an elevator, a curving staircase winding upward free from the walls and banked with flowering plants. My father traveled to England to inspect the paneled rooms he bought before they were shipped. The only exception to his command that everything be English was my bedroom. I had two Early American canopied beds and a highboy. They are now in my granddaughter's bedroom in Boston, looking as beautiful as when I was a child.

The most momentous event of my young life occurred in 1920. It was the day we moved from Morristown to Mayfields, our new stone house in Far Hills, New Jersey. Designed by John Cross, it had a slate roof, stately halls, freestanding staircases, and a paneled library. My room was the only French one, and almost everything in it remains with me today. The Aubusson rug is in the front hall of my apartment, the night table is in a guest room in Maine, and the bed is in the attic there.

My parents were perfectionists, but if they were striving for perfection in their daughter, they were disappointed. By the second grade they recognized I was untalented and graceless. The most expensive tutors did everything they could. Nothing went untried; every attempt failed.

I was given fencing lessons to improve my poise, but I couldn't hold on to the sword.

My parents immediately switched me to ballet, but after two lessons my teacher resigned.

A large piano was moved in next, but it was discovered I was tone deaf.

Next came knitting lessons, but it would have taken me a lifetime to produce a pair of socks.

I fared no better at ballroom dancing.

The most wasted efforts were the journeys to Europe. We toured in a Hispano-Suiza with two bodies, one with a hard top for town, the other with a collapsible top for the country. This was followed by a second car bearing our luggage. We visited all the historic châteaux, museums, and cathedrals, the magnificent country houses of all our foreign friends — and I never learned anything. I kept my eyes closed the whole time.

I never learned a thing at school and never tried to. Somehow I made it through the eighth grade at Miss Chapin's, and that meant it was time for Foxcroft, where my education ended. My principal accomplishment there was the method I developed for avoiding exams: pressing a tender spot on my nose, I would get a nosebleed. I am sure I am the only girl who ever left Foxcroft without a certificate. If school does play a part in one's qualifications as a decorator, then I am certainly the least qualified individual ever to venture past a sign saying "To the Trade."

At one point the school authorities were so alarmed they suggested I see a psychiatrist. He asked me, "Do you like school?" and Mother answered, "No." He asked, "Do you like riding?" and Mother answered, "Yes." He asked, "Do you believe in God?" and Mother answered, "No." Finally he told me that I could leave. He asked Mother to stay.

As for my relationships with boys, my brothers' goal was to embarrass me. When I was invited to my first dance, I knew I wouldn't be sent flowers, so I sent them to myself. Unfortunately, Gory spotted my handwriting on the card and viciously announced, "Sister sent herself flowers!" The first time I was kissed, I immediately informed my parents that I was going to have a baby.

Determined that I would succeed as a debutante, Mother and her secretary planned my coming-out party for months. It was held at the Pierre after the 1927 Harvard-Yale game. We had Lester Lanin at one end of the ballroom and Meyer Davis at the other. The champagne bottles had ribbons and fresh ivy wound around them.

The next summer I went again to Paris, but when I entered the family apartment this time, eighteen years old and feeling very grown up, something stirred in me. I wandered through the rooms, looking at everything in a new, more careful way. I marveled at the carved fruitwood tables, Aubusson carpet, and painted furniture. I was discovering something I knew was important, though I couldn't have said why. This time my eyes were open, and so was my heart.

Returning home, I realized that a deep, abiding belief in all things inherited, and all things of lasting quality, had been awoken in me. I was finally beginning to understand beauty and the role it would play in my life. I have a photograph taken of me at that time. There is a look of confidence in my eyes that is new. The girl in the picture looks very much as my own daughters looked when they were eighteen. And she looks very much as my mother looks in a small yellowed snapshot taken of her at about the same age.

My parents' goal for me was marriage to a Harvard man, and then only if he were a member of the Porcellian Club, which elected fewer than ten members a year. Candidates were invited by Mother to a black-tie dinner party at our house in New York. I didn't have to ask any of the men where they had gone to college or what club they had belonged to. They were all at least three years out of Harvard and settled in good banking jobs. I thought they were ancient. They thought they were gods.

For the first hour, I was in a state of dread. Thank heavens one of the men saw it as his duty to make an effort with me. He was Harry Parish. He was wonderful looking, with blue eyes and broad shoulders, and I soon learned that he was gentle and sweet as well as perfectly mannered, and best of all, we both loved big band music. This led naturally to dinner and dancing at the Casino in Central Park. I knew I would marry him.

Another family trip to Europe had been planned

for that summer and I was miserable about leaving. In Paris I slyly bought small flower drawings, odd teacups, and beribboned porcelain bowls for "our" house. When I returned home it became apparent to my family and Harry's that formal discussions would have to be held.

Harry was very proper, his parents even more so. Mine were racy by comparison. Harry's were brought up in a ponderous way in enormous houses. One was the old Henri Bendel on 57th Street. When I first knew Harry, his family was living with his grandfather, Henry Parish, the president of the Bank of New York, which was founded by my great-grandfather, Lucius Tuckerman. Henry Parish didn't believe in telephones. All business was transacted in person or through messengers. His house on the corner of Madison Avenue and 79th Street was one of the grandest in New York. The Parish children learned to roller-skate on an Aubusson I later inherited.

Harry and I were married on Saint Valentine's Day, 1930. Everything would have been perfect if I hadn't come down with chicken pox. Walking down the aisle, I only thought, "Thank God for the veil." At the reception at our house butlers passed caviar and dainty sandwiches filled with nasturtiums, watercress, and crab. I spent my wedding night in the care of a doctor.

My parents provided a beautiful house for Harry and me at 146 East End Avenue. It was done by Mrs. Brown of McMillen — with Mother's help and suggestions. Wedding presents supplied the furnishings. We had to buy only one upholstered chair, at Macy's, and I was appalled at having to pay forty dollars. (I still have the chair in my apartment.) We had a couple who worked for us and a laundress twice a week, and we slept on big square pillowcases with monograms so prominent I often woke up with DMP stamped on my cheek.

Three months after our wedding I was told I would be having a baby. Little Harry's first word

The cool, flower-strewn living room in the summer house.

was "birdy," a signal to move to the country. We found a small farmhouse in Far Hills, a thing of wonder. It was yellow with white shutters, a picket fence, and apple trees all around. Twenty-one and full of confidence, I wasn't the least bit afraid of what people might say about my taste. When the Parishes offered to give us furniture from their town house, I chose a suite of black ebony, covered in Aubusson tapestry. There was a carpet to match, the one the Parish children used to skate over. I then did something no one had ever heard of: I painted the ebony furniture white. Harry's mother would choke before allowing that the effect was "interesting." But I knew what I was after, and I was delighted with the result. Ficus trees stood in the corners of the living room — no one had seen one before. Mattress ticking and damask tablecloths with the Parish crest, which I painted scarlet, were sewn into curtains. Mrs. Parish wondered why I hadn't left the windows bare until the real curtains arrived.

In our bedroom I painted the floor, another daring innovation. I wanted it cherry red with white diamonds, and Harry spent much of the summer on hands and knees, making sure the diamonds came out right. I had the mantel made from structural blocks of Steuben glass applied to the wall, which I had painted red just there. Taffeta flowed down from a crown. Now of course hangings are something no one can go to sleep without. The first night Harry and I kept the lights on because it was so beautiful.

Some people were horrified by what I'd done. Someone said, "Well, I guess you will always be different, Sister." But I had accomplished something original. I knew it and they knew it. Soon friends came seeking advice. It never occurred to me that I wasn't qualified to give it. The living room at the Essex Hunt Club was looking a bit down-at-heel — could I do something about it? I decided to replace the stiff masculine furniture with comfortable upholstered sofas and chairs. I donated a coffee table of my own to make the place seem more like home and had mirrors installed on either side of the

Harry and Sister with "Little Harry," Apple, and D.B., early 1940s.

mantel so people could see themselves dancing. It was a terrifying experience, but nobody said anything horrible. In fact, the reviews were positive. The mirrors are still there.

A short time after, Senator Frelinghuysen of New Jersey, a friend, told me of a restaurant that needed some decorating help. It was called Howard Johnson's. I dressed the waitresses in aqua, painted the walls aqua, did the placemats in aqua. I must have thought aqua was chic, though I haven't touched the color since. But I still have a love for Howard Johnson's.

I had never known a woman who worked. Certainly not a married woman, and most definitely not a married woman with a child. I had decorated the Hunt Club for pleasure and Howard Johnson's for little more than free ice cream. But the Crash had come, and earning money, if not socially acceptable, was at least useful.

Harry arrived home from work at Loeb, Rhoades on Christmas Eve 1933 with the news that his salary

had been cut. Without telling him, I went to work. It never occurred to me to start anywhere but at the top, so my first move was to arrive unannounced in the New York office of the president of Stroheim & Romann, the fabrics firm. I hung around until finally a man, the head of this important company, acknowledged me. I told him the whole sad story — Harry's cut salary, a baby, a dog, a cat, and a goat to feed. He looked frenzied and said, "Young lady, what is it exactly that you want?" I said, "I want to buy materials, I want to be a decorator, and I want to be a decorator this afternoon." He tried to convince me that I would never make a go of it, but he finally gave me an account with his firm, then begged me to get out. I did, but not before calling to find out how baby Harry was. Leaving the building with the samples I imagined I needed to get started, I encountered my first problem. I didn't know how to work the revolving door.

I suppose I was what is today called a working woman, though I never thought of myself as that. The odd thing is that we could have gotten along without my working. We were supposed to be penniless, but we still had a cook, an outside man, and a nursemaid.

I had become a decorator, but I still hadn't the nerve to tell Harry. A few weeks later I rented a fourteen-by-fourteen-foot room in Far Hills for thirty-five dollars a month. I went to work the first morning with a pencil, a piece of paper, a wicker chair, and a wicker desk. I painted the room white myself and hung out a sign in my own terrible handwriting that said *Mrs. Henry Parish II, Interiors*. When I showed the place to Harry, he missed the sign and I had to explain twice before he understood that this was my shop. There was a long silence, then a smile of admiration. Neither of us imagined that I would one day be working for people like our friends the Charles Engelhards, decorating their Dutch Colonial house in Johannesburg, labeling bed linen number 71 to go in the closet of room 71.

Harry's family definitely did not approve. When

his uncle and aunt, Henry and Susie Parish, learned I had become a decorator, they left a sizable sum, which had been due Harry, to Susie's cousin, Mrs. Franklin Roosevelt. They concluded that even marrying a Democrat was preferable to marrying a woman in trade.

The first person to enter the shop was Mrs. Anderson Fowler, the daughter of a family acquaintance. She trusted me completely, though I didn't know much more than she did. I put a curved sofa in the bay window of her country house. That was considered extraordinary.

I did not need a decorator's manual; the arrangement of furniture and a feeling for lighting and color came to me naturally. I just knew that the tables should be all the same height so the lamps would be at the same level. I did do some research on valances, but that was all. Then as now, I did not have a reason for everything I did and was not afraid to simply feel my way.

People in Far Hills liked not having to go to New York for their decorating needs. In the office there was only myself and a secretary who came part-time from the inn across the street. She was as new at this as I was, but she did organize me. I hadn't a clue about money. I'm a little better today, but not much. I know what things cost, but as far as running a business . . . Sometimes I wonder how we're still going.

I had not gone to school, read any books, or served an apprenticeship, and I am still hopeless with that thing called a scale rule. And yet I was a decorator. That is because I had a decorator's eye and instinct. There must be twenty thousand decorators in New York today. They've all studied at Parsons or some other school. They can draw a floor plan and they know the history of furniture, but that doesn't seem to be what's necessary. What's necessary is to have it in you. I don't care how much studying you've done — if you haven't got it in you, you won't be able to put it across.

Money isn't the answer either. You have to give part of yourself; part of yourself is what really makes it home. I love wherever I am because I make it home, even a hotel room. I move the furniture around, bring along a few favorite coverlets. You can never achieve anything in a house unless you have things that have been passed down and that you find a place for yourself.

With the war nearing, Harry was sent for training at a naval base in Florida. Our lives and those of our three children — Apple and D.B. were born in 1933 and 1935 — were turned upside down. After eight years in business, I closed and moved down South with Harry. When he left for the Pacific on a carrier, I took an apartment in New York, did Red Cross canteen work, and joined a firm called Budget Decorators. It was 1941, I was thirty-one, and I brought in all the business. I resigned after two years.

With the war over and Harry back safe, I sailed to England in 1948 with my old Foxcroft classmate Bunny Mellon to discuss a possible business tie-up with Colefax & Fowler. They sent me furniture that I sold in New York, and I sent them things like tassels that they had trouble producing in England after the war. But the arrangement was soon stopped because of currency restrictions.

By championing the so-called English country house look — chintz, needlework, the most sumptuous upholstery — Colefax & Fowler became the most influential decorating firm in Britain. John Fowler was the motor. When I think of John I think of impossibly detailed curtains with dressmaker furbelows, and of rooms that are romantic without being sentimental or bitsy, a look that is very difficult to achieve. The man himself was unassuming — as English as Billy Baldwin was American. Working in New York, Billy designed in a modern idiom without abandoning the past. He loved plain curtains, plaster lamps, straw, rattan, and bamboo. He and John liked luxury that didn't shout.

One of John's disciples is Mario Buatta. Mario's wonderful. He calls me up and says, "What have you done lately that I can copy?" I adore him because he's so fantastic at advertising himself and at that thing called licensing. I've been to three cocktail parties in my life that had to do with business, and I envy the decorators who go to three in an afternoon. The public thing, I'm just not made for it.

John's partner was my American friend Nancy Lancaster. As her guest at Ditchley Park, she could take you to any house you wanted to see. At Ditchley the walls were hung with nineteenth-century damask Nancy dared to bleach. And she approached the bathrooms as real rooms, filling them with furniture, an original idea at the time. At Haseley Court, where she later lived, Nancy sat at one end of the dining table in a Queen Anne wing chair, slipcovered in chintz and with pillows thrown in its hollows. Except for the man sitting opposite in a chair that was the twin to hers, all the other guests were given tufted William IV leather ones. I always found the contrast amusing.

While I relished my work, by 1962, managing alone was wearing me out. I had been at it solo for twenty-eight years. Albert Hadley joined me from McMillen at this time, and in two years he was my partner. I didn't interview anyone else and didn't need to. It is no secret that I never would have accomplished all the things I have without him. We have had hard times, we have had fun, we have experienced real torture, and we have had disagreements, but all of that comes with the job. When we are summoned to view a house, he always accompanies me. If it's hopeless, I become terribly fragile and say, "Please take me home, Albert. I'm not feeling well." Albert has always stood with me, beside me, behind me. He is always at hand.

Among the regrettable "rewards" of the celebrity I have accumulated have been invitations to lecture. Statesmen, children, my housekeeper have given me advice: stand on a copy of *Time* magazine for confidence; if you get a run in your stocking, don't look down to see how bad it is; take a big swig; take a Valium.

One of my worst summers was spent rehearsing a speech. No sleep, just worry. I decided my only hope was to devote a large part of my days practicing in my church at Dark Harbor. The first time I rose to the pulpit my Pekingese sat in the front pew. As I prepared to address the empty church where I've been going all my life with my children, their children, my friends, my dogs, I thought, What is there to all the excitement? But with a large clock and my text in absurdly oversized type in hand, I hadn't a word to say. When I finally uttered something, my Pekes let out a terrible moan.

People always question me about trends. From the beginning, I never followed them. If I was aware of trends I didn't care, for I believed then, as I do now, that rooms should be timeless and very personal. I didn't set out to achieve a particular style or develop a "look," because I knew that every person's life differs from every other, and that all needs are therefore different. And yet what I do has often been referred to as having a look — the Undecorated Look. Now that is certainly what I like, but I am not sure it isn't because I don't know any better. In any case, if my Undecorated Look has meant rooms that are comfortable and friendly, imaginative and warm, expressing a certain continuity, then I feel I have accomplished a great deal.

Some years ago, Albert and I were delighted when patchwork quilts, four-poster beds, painted floors, rag rugs, painted valances, and knitted throws were first listed among the "innovations" of our firm. (Today it seems we can't sell a sofa unless it's got some sort of shawl hanging over the end of it.) The list sounds old-fashioned, and certainly no decorator wants to be that. But we understood, all the same, that innovation is often the ability to reach into the past and bring back what is good, what is beautiful, what is useful, what is lasting.

At the start of my career I instinctively set out to make some old ideas popular again, and after sixty years I am pleased to see that they still work. It is like the pleasure I feel when I remember the day at Dark Harbor, long ago, when I learned to tie all the ship's knots. Even now they hold tight in my memory, and I think they have helped not just in keeping my boat fast, but in keeping my life fast.

A Past With Design

by Albert Hadley

SOMETIME BETWEEN MIDNIGHT AND DAWN on November 11, 1920, a son was born to Elizabeth Lois Meguiar Hadley in the little country town of Springfield, Tennessee. The father of the child was Albert Livingston Hadley, the owner of a farm implements and buggy company in this prosperous town, some thirty miles from Nashville, the capital of the state. Springfield was the center for tobacco farming in Robertson County.

Two years had passed since the Armistice had been signed and World War I had ended. This day was charged with celebration. There was merrymaking and dancing in the town square by day, and at night the sky was ablaze with fireworks set off to the accompaniment of music by the firehouse band. To witness the sight, Bert held his son in his arms at the open window of the room where he had just been born.

I am told that my eyes blinked and a tiny smile crossed my face as the night sky blazed in colored light. I like to think that that is true.

Albert Hadley, 1987.

My mother grew up on a large working farm about five miles north of Nashville on the Gallatin Pike, the main road linking the capital to the small rural towns in the direction of Kentucky. Her father, Alexander Franklin Meguiar, had married Maggie Hillard, one of the five vivacious Hillard girls. When the high-spirited Hillard girls, so good at capturing a small boy's attention, visited Broadmoor, the Nashville farm where my grandparents settled, I would beg them to tell me their stories of war and peace. The war stories conveyed the destruction and ruin caused by the Civil War, which they had known firsthand. But their peace stories were of foxhunts, quilting parties, and hoopskirted young ladies dancing the Virginia reel with chivalrous young Southern gentlemen. I listened, transfixed.

Broadmoor had a curious appearance, an old house added to many times without regard for architectural merit, but the parlor was magical and mysterious, like a jeweled cave. Above a small black marble mantel hung a tall gold-framed mirror — very much the style for Victorian parlors. The windows had very plain gilded cornices. The walls were covered with a heavy paper whose gold embossing outlined an all-over floral design in cream, tan, brown, and mossy green. All of this had come with the house. Throughout, my grandparents covered the wide floorboards with smooth china matting put down in strips.

In the parlor, a small Turkish rug was laid over the matting in front of the hearth. From a dry goods store in Nashville, my grandmother chose a medium moss-green brocatelle, its pattern highlighted by the glint of gold thread. This she used for the curtains, which she made herself, and to recover some highly carved and ornamental parlor furniture inherited from her parents. Other bits of upholstery and various stools and cushions made no effort to conform to the scheme. But because there was continuity, if you like, to her madness, the room was not a hodgepodge. Rather, her informed daring invested it with a feeling of comfort, quality, and a sort of casual elegance. When the dark louvered shutters were opened — this happened mostly on Sundays — light filtering through heavy lace undercurtains created thick, atmospheric shadows. In the evening, when my aunt Mary practiced Bach on the new upright piano, the glass-shaded lamp on the marble-topped center table was lighted, its pink glow combining with the trembling light cast by the candles on the mantel and on a pair of brackets attached to the piano. I've never forgotten the allure of that room.

Looking back, I realize World War I was hard on my father's family. In January 1918, a contract was signed by the United States government and DuPont for the construction of the world's largest powder plant on 5,600 acres of farmland skirted by a wide bend in the Cumberland River, known as Hadley's Bend. It included property that was the life and livelihood of my ancestors. Within six months, the Old Hickory Smokeless Powder Works was in operation. Four months after that, the plant was producing 700,000 pounds of powder daily.

With their rye and wheat fields pulled up, their houses desolate and vacant, the Hadleys of Hadley's Bend were obliged to start over in a handful of scattered communities. My widowed grandmother Mathilde was among the displaced, giving up the simple, dignified house she and my grandfather Albert received from his father as a wedding present. Called Gretna Green, it was a beautiful house of classical style made of pale pink bricks molded by the hands of slaves, and all the furnishings had come from either Saint Louis or New Orleans by boat. A local newspaper carried this account:

> *How sad it must make [the Hadleys] feel to leave the homes where they were born and have lived such a happy peaceful life. But room must be made for the great powder plant and there is no alternative, they must go, and, going, see their homes pulled to the ground and their crops destroyed.*

Vaucluse in Hadley's Bend, Tennessee, built in 1826 by Albert's great-great-grandfather, Mr. John Livingston Hadley, Sr.

With the signing of the Armistice the same year it was constructed, the factory became redundant. Machinery was sold off to sawmills, tanneries, and other factories. In 1923, part of the property landed back in the hands of DuPont, which built facilities for the manufacture of rayon — which was to change forever how one regarded real silk. From residue produced in the manufacturing of rayon, another even more fascinating material was made— cellophane!

In a child's eye, a cellophane factory couldn't be all bad, especially if one had a relative who worked there. From time to time my father's younger brother, Uncle Howard, would bring me giant rolls of the clear, shiny, jewel-colored, pliable material. I draped cellophane over chair backs, and threw it over tabletops, fascinated with its brilliant colors and light-catching properties. To this day cellophane is for me a festive trip!

By my second birthday, my father had moved the family into a bright, boxy new bungalow in the fast-developing outskirts of Nashville. From the rocky unpaved street one entered through a curvaceous iron and wire gate set in an ornamental fence, the top worked in overlapping scallops. A pair of small umbrella trees planted just inside the gate gave the place a confident air of formality. These magnolias had tall, straight trunks supporting thick branches of waxy green leaves that grew naturally to form a great dome of an umbrella. As a finishing gesture, their trunks were whitewashed up to a height just above my head. The effect was dazzling, a bit of exoticism in our plain neighborhood.

A gravel path took one to wide steps onto the porch that went across the front of the house. There were colorful flower beds, a lawn, a vegetable garden, and a henhouse with roosting poles. After Trixie, my fox terrier, made the Rhode Island Reds and white

Plymouth Rocks scamper, sending feathers flying, I would collect a fistful of the fluffy talismans and stick them in my father's battered old farmer's hat, which I was seldom without. There and then, my fascination with feathers was born.

My creative talents were expanded further when one day I was found quietly engaged in drawing at the foot of the new ivory-painted bed that was part of a suite of furniture my father had bought as a present for the new house. The bed's cane-over-wood head- and footboards, topped by urn-shaped finials, were too great a temptation. I couldn't resist filing every hole of the canework with the bright blue of an indelible pencil. I don't remember what the punishment was, but my discovery of that color made it worth it. I began to see blue everywhere — in the morning glories in the garden, in my grandmother's everyday willowware, in the cobalt finger bowls lined up on the serving table.

Then came red — this, however, in the form of a long strand of bright red cut-glass beads worn by my favorite next-door neighbor, Mrs. Epps. On occasion I would be allowed to hold them in my hands and be dazzled by their fiery light. I don't remember wearing them around my neck except once, and that was when I was given an "Indian suit" for Christmas. It was not just a suit, it was the whole she-bang — a fringed and beaded buckskin suit with matching moccasins and a fantastic multicolored feathered headdress that only the Big Chief could wear. I was in a state of tribal joy in that costume and I remember that the red beads added magic. At that point, red became my favorite color.

By the time my sister was born we had moved to a house in Nashville, so that I could attend elementary school in town. I may have only been approaching six, but no one could persuade me that the new house wasn't ugly. It was constructed of a new building material — cast cement — simulating rusticated stone. Chickens and a dog and a cat negotiated peace in our yard, but charm did not enter into it.

In summer, at least, morning glories shimmying up the guide wires enveloped the entire façade of the house, screening its porch from a street on which all the merchants — the baker, the grocer, the iceman — passed in big wagons. The thick vegetation also made of the open porch a cool green cave where my friends and I played. Deep drifts of four-o'clocks planted along the foundation of the shady north side of the house waited until that hour in the afternoon to open, their petals unfolding into flowers the size of silver dollars. I immediately included their bright pink color — the same one Elsa Schiaparelli would many years later call "shocking" — in my palette of favorites. Things were looking up.

Ready for a powwow, about age two.

Opposite top: The Buggy and Farm Implements Store pre-1920. A. L. Hadley is standing at the left in the photograph.

Opposite bottom: The "Garden Club" ladies wore hats, 1929. Lois Hadley is standing at the extreme left in the photograph.

At root a farmboy, my father seized the chance to return to country life in 1929, when a big farm machinery firm offered him a job as a salesman. Mother chose the plans of her dream house from the pages of a magazine. It was built using glazed brick the color of hand-churned butter; it had white trim, a shingle roof, green-black shutters, and gables that made one think of Hansel and Gretel. The interior finishes were done by a troupe of animated Italian artisans who did breathtaking work but who had to be closely supervised — otherwise they got carried away by their own Mediterranean enthusiasm. For example, without ever consulting anyone, they covered the bedroom walls on the second floor with plaster mixed with great quantities of sand. Finished, the walls had the texture of rough sandpaper. But the advantage, the workers told my mother, was that the color was worked right in: the walls would *never* need painting! Despair!!

Downstairs was another story. When the artisans learned of my mother's preference for smooth walls of definite color, they gave me my first real lesson in the art of interior decoration. Mother showed them a panel of the new curtains that were to hang in the living room, a dull green cloth woven with vines and leaves and shot with gold thread that highlighted the design, a throwback no doubt to the parlor in her parents' house. The painters were in their element, painting the smooth plaster a creamy mustard color. Over this they went to work with wads of cheesecloth dipped in a soft green paint, smearing and patting and rubbing. The result was a warmly glowing room of translucent shimmering color. I was enthralled.

Everything about the house interested me. I was always trying to persuade my mother to go a bit further in her decorating schemes. Sometimes, I won. As my taste was more dramatic, I somehow managed to banish the ivory of her now old bedroom

suite under a coat of apple-green paint, then picked out the beading and garlands in gold, obliterating all traces of my lovely blue squiggles.

I enjoyed tagging along with my mother and one or two of her friends on what they called their "antiquing" days. Buzzing through the countryside in her bright blue sedan, they would walk up to the front door of any house that looked promising, knock hard, and ask the owners straight out if they had anything they wanted to sell. More often than not, they did, simple but pretty things no longer used or treasured. If the day's take was furniture too big for the backseat of the car, my father would have to return later with a truck to bring the treasures home. It became quite a game. In this way, a house that started out rather sparsely furnished became one of considerable interest and charm.

As a result of these early experiences, what I really like to do, even now, is rescue things from people's attics, working with favorite possessions and reorganizing what is already there, filling in where necessary and upgrading quality when appropriate. "Antiquing" today is quite a different story.

While I was still in high school, where I was beginning to study architecture until my mathematical deficiencies discouraged me, I managed to have a summer job as a salesman at Bradford's, one of the best furniture stores in Nashville. That gave me my first valuable experience dealing with the public. Selling sofas, tables, and chairs, I was able to give advice to the customers and suggest ways to use their purchases when they got home — if they would listen. My authority came from the pages of *House & Garden*, *House Beautiful*, and *Vogue*. I learned about the great tastemakers of the time, from Elsie de Wolfe, who is always credited with inventing the profession of interior decorating, to all of the prominent New York decorators of the day. I was especially taken by the high style of the "modern Merlin of decoration" as he was billed in the pages of *House Beautiful* magazine — William Pahlmann. He was the top-flight decorator for Lord & Taylor.

Page 32: Albert's barn in Dark Harbor, Maine, 1968.

Page 33: The silver tea paper sitting room in the New York apartment, 1992.

Meeting A. Herbert Rodgers when I was seventeen years old confirmed what I already knew: I wanted to be a decorator. Mr. Rodgers was the most prominent decorator in the South. He had a glamorous shop and workroom on West End Avenue in Nashville. He was famous for his bold color schemes and dramatic effects. His feeling for French architecture and decoration came from having served in France during the war. An addition to the sturdy brick building that housed his business was a square, high-ceilinged room with tall arched windows looking out onto West End Avenue. Inside, all was magic and beauty. Hanging in the center of the lofty space was a huge eighteenth-century crystal-and-ormulu French chandelier. There was a constant play of reflected light; breezes produced a soft, musical, tinkling sound. Mr. Rodgers had glazed the walls of this memorable space a deep peacock blue, picked out the trim in white, and anchored the room with his signature black skirting boards. Masses of huge gardenia plants filled simple clay pots, and ornamental trees practically brushed the ceiling. Finally, the highly polished Versailles-style parquet creaked — loudly and intentionally. Mr. Rodgers had achieved this effect of an old floor by dousing the newly laid floor with water.

After graduating from high school, I studied art and design at Peabody College in Nashville, leaving after two years in order to gain some additional working experience before being drafted. After a year at the Period Furniture Company, where I held the same sort of job as I had had at Bradford's, I accepted Mr. Rodgers's offer to work as his assistant. I was involved in everything from assisting Mr. Rodgers with schemes and clients to deliveries and installations, a completely nourishing apprenticeship. Even then, though, my sole ambition was to get to New York. But the war came, and I went.

As a corporal in the 861st Aviation Engineer Battalion stationed in England, I spent my one-day leaves every week in London. Headquarters for American servicemen was a club in Piccadilly called Rainbow Corner. One of the volunteers, Lady Cavendish — Adele Astaire, Fred Astaire's sister — introduced me to a woman I had also read about in *House & Garden*, Constance Spry, who was famous for her exotic flower arrangements and who had been extensively publicized when she had flowers flown from England to France to decorate Elsie de Wolfe's famous Circus Party at Versailles.

I was also introduced to Emma Shields, who in her decorating shop dedicated herself to white. Sent by one of the ladies at Rainbow Corner, I was greeted at the front door by a small woman with delicate features and gentle motions, wearing a dark blue dress of heavy crepe, cut to discreetly emphasize her tiny waist. The deep V-neckline was without jewels, but her classic black pumps had enormous cut-steel buckles. Her three-quarter-length sleeves fell loosely and ended in an explosion of iridescent blue-black feathers. A second door opened and we were in a vast white space punctuated by enormous rubber plants. The walls were white, the floors were white, masses of old English oak furniture had been heavily pickled, and where fabric was needed, it too was white. The quality of everything was superb. There were simple clear glass lamps — bases purchased from a chemist's shop fitted with large pleated paper shades. The only color came from an assortment of American Indian rugs, all in clear, vibrant colors and simple, uncomplicated designs.

When the war was over, I came to New York and enrolled in a six-week summer course at the Parsons School of Design. At the end of the course I was offered a scholarship, so I stayed to finish the regular three-year program. My experience working for furniture companies, time spent with Mr. Rodgers in his studio with on-the-job exposure to some of the most beautiful houses and rooms in and around Nashville, plus all that I'd seen and done in London, definitely gave me a head start on my formal education in design. Van Day Truex, the president of Parsons, had himself been trained in design by the school's founder, Frank Alvah Parsons. Parsons was

The White Rabbit blew three blasts on the trumpet, and then unrolled the parchment-scroll, and read as follows:

"I have not yet, indeed, thought of a remedy for luxury..."

The Duchess of York

"elegance is refusal"
DIANA VREELAND

DON'T FORGET

ZAP

a contemporary of Edith Wharton and the architect/designer Ogden Codman.

The school also advanced the cause of modernism. Van Day Truex had known Jean-Michel Frank from the days when he headed Parsons's Paris branch, and it was Frank's designs and philosophy that he borrowed and popularized. Van Truex's feeling was "If something is good once, it's always good." When he had something compelling he wanted you to know, he clamped one of his huge, expressive paws on the knob of your shoulder, then spoke through bared and clenched teeth. With eyes that widened to set his dictum in italics, what he often said was "Provide less, provide better." Or, "Mother Nature" — *nay-tcha* as he pronounced it in the middle-Atlantic accent he cultivated — "she's always the best designer." Or, "Outside of scientific advances, everything has been done."

Parsons offered not only scholastic studio experience, but also exposed students to some of the best professionals of the time. There were field trips to visit some of the most glamorous interiors belonging to people of highly cultivated tastes, for the most part friends and acquaintances of Mr. Truex. There were rich experiences, to be continued even after I graduated in 1949. In the early autumn of that same year, when Mr. Truex returned from a summer abroad with students in Europe, I was asked to return to Parsons to teach. It was the close association with the president and the talented director of the Interior Design Department, Harold Guy, that made the experience of the next five years invaluable. I loved working with the young creative minds of the students, and suspect that I learned more from them than they from me. But the time had come to practice what I preached and begin my career.

I resigned from Parsons in 1954 to set out on my own as a decorator, working out of a small studio apartment on East 57th Street.

My business was successful, but I could hardly refuse, after a few years, joining McMillen Inc., the leading decorating firm in the country, when Mrs. Archibald Brown, the company's founder and direc-tor, approached me in 1957. The McMillen style was unimpeachably grand yet never heavy-handed. With their overtones of European propriety and atmosphere of intellectual coolness, rooms were filled with pedigreed furniture spanning a number of periods, old wallpaper and exotic materials, displays of rare porcelains, curtains trimmed out in the most sophisticated way, and the dressiest silks, chintzes, brocades, and velvets. Attention was paid to historical correctness.

Mrs. Brown was as private as she was professional. The charm bracelet that she was never without was like the bell on a cat — you always heard her coming. Her employees suspected she wore it to avoid the awkwardness she was afraid might arise from someone encountering her unawares. Mrs. Brown kept, and made the rest of us keep, strict hours. She felt that anything that couldn't be accomplished in a normal business day could wait. Certainly there was no lazing around the office after five o'clock trading ideas with colleagues.

One of the most important projects I worked on while at McMillen was with Ethel Smith: the restoration of Rosedown Plantation in St. Francisville, Louisiana. With my knowledge and love of Southern houses of the period, it was an exciting project for me. It was a gigantic undertaking, but when we finished rehabilitating the ravishing furniture original to the house, and paying strict attention to details such as the re-embroidering of the punkah over the dining room table, following its original eagle design by Audubon, Rosedown became known as a brilliant example of Louis Philippe period decoration in this country.

Despite all the opportunities I enjoyed at McMillen during my five years with the firm, I felt stifled. In the end, Eleanor McMillen Brown, the least manipulative person in the world, supported my decision to leave. There was no acrimony.

The first person I called with the news was Van Day Truex, a great friend of Mrs. Brown. That same night he sat next to Mrs. Henry Parish at a dinner party. She was threatening to retire unless she found someone with whom to share her responsibilities. The rest is decorating history.

Just as Sister Parish, with her warm manner and ever-present Pekingese, Yummy, in her arms, was the exact opposite of Mrs. Brown, so Mrs. Henry Parish II, as her business was known, was the exact opposite of McMillen. Sis's operation was completely unstructured and, even she would say, unprofessional. An assistant, a secretary, and a bookkeeper were the only people on the payroll. Clients were mostly friends, or friends of friends. Her social connections counted for a lot. There were no estimates. Everything was done on trust. All of the design work was done in her head — nothing on paper. In any case, Sis didn't need a lot of backup. In those days, she traveled directly to the job with her curtain-maker and upholsterer and worked everything out on site.

From the time I started, Sis never spoke of retirement again. She liked having someone ten years younger spurring her on. Her work for President and Mrs. Kennedy at the White House was coming to an end, but I did have the privilege to be involved in the decoration of the small dining room on the main floor. Designing the curtains for this room was my first assignment in our new venture together.

One project that year that made a great impression on me was the drawing room in the Georgetown house of Mrs. Robert Charles, then Oatsie Leiter. Another commission that first year was Mrs. Vincent Astor's house in Maine. The furniture plans for the Astor project fell to me, and I did them the way I had always been trained, meaning that the precise position of every sofa, table, and lamp was decided in the office, well in advance of the installation. Sis wasn't intimidated by my approach, but she didn't understand it, either. We were both in Maine when the delivery truck finally arrived with all the furniture. With her propelling them, tables and chairs

scooted across the floor in an entirely different configuration from my plans. This was the first time I had actually witnessed Sis's baroque, freewheeling style of working. I was completely entranced.

With more commissions than either of us had expected, the firm grew quickly.

If early in our collaboration Sis had heard of modernism, it didn't interest her very much, but I was the disciple. Such innovations as lacquered walls, modern lighting, even classic Oriental tables bound in raffia and dipped in enamel paint were included in my design vocabulary. With my influence, the backgrounds of the rooms the company decorated began to change. For instance, in the London apartment of the Charles Englehards, the walls were in a buttercup yellow, high-gloss paint, an innovation at the time. This was the background for an eclectic mix of good eighteenth-century French and English furniture and objects. Even though the schemes were traditional, the setting was fresh, clean, bright, and up-to-date. It was here, for the first time, that we used fabrics of our own designs, which had been produced in America. They were of stylized documentary patterns in surprisingly bright colors, all printed on cotton — a definite departure from established English tastes. Not only have we continued to produce fabric designs for many individual projects, we have produced custom-designed furniture, lamps, rugs, and accessories, working with artists and artisans to create objects of classical inspiration, but pure twentieth-century spirit. This was the beginning of a fresh and slightly irreverent point of view about contemporary interiors that we have maintained in the work of our office through the years. Our role is to help make dreams come true, and in the process heed the advice of our friend of many years ago, Diana Vreeland, who, when she was told of one of our new assignments, said: "Give 'em what they never knew they wanted!"

Arrivals

THE ENTRY HALL, a hyphen between exterior and interior worlds . . .

*

setting the stage . . .

*

striking the right note of familiarity: tennis rackets lying about
(striking the wrong note: family photographs) . . .

*

on and around the console table: a key and mail tray, pad and pencils,
gardenia plants in straw cachepots, a mirror framed by suitable sconces,
a basket below for your favorite animal . . .

*

umbrellas and walking sticks in containers of tole or marble, glass
or porcelain . . .

*

wood-framed furniture with leather, tapestry, other strong coverings . . .

*

classic in a town entrance: parquet, strips of watered mirror . . .

*

a lantern rather than a chandelier . . .

*

botanical, animal, and other decorative prints . . .

*

the dry, French, intellectual approach: tapestries and family portraits, Caen
stone and marble, iron and brawny hall chairs . . .

*

a windowed alcove with a telephone and telephone table . . .

"YOU DON'T REALLY NEED TO GO SHOPPING" *(left)*

The entrance hall of Mrs. Parish's New York maisonette, formerly Gloria Swanson's, has a bright vivacious quality while at the same time incorporating all the elements of a formal entry: table, mirror, clock, flowers, letter tray, and sets of chairs and pictures that each assumes its proper place.

Walls covered in linen painted with freehand stripes are crowned with an elaborate Directoire border in the same coral, cream, and blue of the Bessarabian rug, laid over bleached oak parquet. Flanking a Regency mirror, the chinoiserie decorations of its black lacquer frame picked out in gold, English nineteenth-century paintings on glass depict the Three Graces. The console, giddy with whorls and carved with five bracket platforms meant to display garniture, and side chairs done in cocoa-colored silk, their stylized wedge backs embraced by serpents, are eighteenth-century Italian. Mrs. Parish capriciously topped the clock in the form of a rusticated column with "a finial off some curtains."

People who make a game of charting how Mrs. Parish gives an old possession new life will recognize the Russian chandelier from her former dining room on 79th Street. As she herself says, "The only reason these things are here is because I had them. I didn't buy anything new. What I like is that everything in the hall has a meaning for me. It belonged to my mother, like the vase. Or it reminds me of a friend. Or I found it amusing. You don't really need to go shopping. You make do with what you have."

A STYLE-SETTER'S HUDSON RIVER STAIR HALL

The English and American dog pictures crowded gallery-style on a curving stair wall in a plain but handsome William Delano house up a hill from the Hudson launched a fashion for the paintings that, many years later, is still not exhausted.

Having mounted a gently winding gravel drive and crossed a wide courtyard, visitors find themselves standing in a hall with a view, framed by French doors, across the library to a terrace on the other side of the house. To the left the space widens, opening into a large stair hall with a low Louis XV table almost a yard square, a delicately looped iron balustrade, and a bar behind shutter doors. Plaster walls were painted a misty mushroom color to tie in with the worn marble floor, and an English longcase clock is flanked by musician-monkeys on porcelain elephant stands as well as by portraits: more dogs.

Centered by an eighteenth-century French lantern, the hall did not take on much decoration because it didn't need it—the very personal and by now famous collection of dog pictures offers plenty of entertainment. "Queen Victoria not only owned numerous dogs, but started the precedent for the commissioning and collecting of dog paintings. This apparently became the rage. . . ."

AMERICAN GEORGIAN *(preceding page)*

Mrs. Parish nods when Albert Hadley describes Annette de la Renta as having "the greatest taste of any American woman of her generation," an estimation formed in the 1960s when they worked together in Katonah, New York, on a Federal-style house. In the hall, lilac walls, an American Empire sofa, and a Chippendale mirror made reference to the look John Fowler called "pleasing decay."

"It was very unselfconscious," says Albert Hadley, "and yet every effort was made to make sure it looks that way."

"NATURE IS MY RELIGION" *(above)*

A formidable horticultural enthusiast, Enid Annenberg Haupt was not destined to have a decorator. Until she enlisted Parish-Hadley to help with her Park Avenue penthouse in the mid-1980s, she had always arranged her own apartments and houses, to spectacular effect.

Parish-Hadley's idea was that a new leaf had to be turned now that Mrs. Haupt's extraordinary collection of Impressionist and Postimpressionist paintings had merged with her brother's. She nevertheless had held on to a Vuillard screen depicting one of the artist's favorite motifs, the place Ventimille in Paris, and a suite of grisaille-and-gold Tiepolo frescoes transferred to canvas from a Venetian palace. Client and designers agreed that the penthouse should have a light elegant mix of mostly French, Italian, and English furniture. The living room was glazed a pale peachy beige, the hall, where lady's slippers from Mrs. Haupt's Greenwich greenhouses are often placed on the staircase one to a step, was painted by Robert Jackson in great blocks of cream and sienna that are meant to suggest marble but not simulate it. Claiming never to have had curtains, only plants and pictures, Mrs. Haupt indulged an old fantasy for unlined silk taffeta at the windows.

Living Rooms

THE LIVING ROOM, family and friends . . .

*

hearth and home . . .

*

if comfortable for forty, comfortable for four . . .

*

the off-limits drawing room vs. the lived-in living room . . .

*

anyplace else but here: the telephone and television . . .

*

the brittle beauty of a baby grand, the frank form of an upright . . .

*

animated decoration sparking animated conversation . . .

*

a leather-wrapped table for playing poker, taking tea . . .

*

the dearest, most elaborate stuffs in the house . . .

*

enough free surfaces for putting things down . . .

*

the power of decoration to civilize . . .

*

flowers that have never seen a florist . . .

*

substantial rather than pincushion-sized pillows . . .

*

seating groups that interact, leaving no one out in the cold . . .

FOURTEEN STORIES ABOVE PARK AVENUE, ROOM TO TALK *(right)*

Because entertaining is such a big part of Mr. and Mrs. Henry Grunwald's lives, all the furniture in their coolly restrained living room is precisely arranged to make dialogue natural and easy.

Neutral walls and plain curtains were chosen as the backdrop for Greek and Egyptian antiquities. The furniture is a mixture of Louis XVI armchairs in their original, muted tapestry and the finest custom-designed soft seating. Notwithstanding the moirés, satins, and giltwood bergère, Mrs. Grunwald had said, "The last thing I want is a room where people are terrified to put their feet up."

A PILLAR OF SOCIETY *(following page)*

One of Washington's most distinguished, old-guard hostesses lives in a mid-nineteenth-century Georgetown house with a drawing room done in a palette of clear colors. Ivory walls and flame-colored silk curtains form the background for an eclectic mix of English, Continental, and Oriental furniture.

PLAIN GEOMETRY

This Gracie Square apartment recounts the ambitions and nesting requirements of a successful Wall Street investment banker of the boom years of the last decade. "Nothing earlier than the early twentieth century," the man had said. A disciple of Jean-Michel Frank, Gary Hager, working with colleague David McMahon, saw in the job the opportunity to create a wealth of custom-made furnishings and special finishes.

But Mr. Hager first dedicated himself to "the thorough and systematic replacement of unworthy detail." The simple Art Deco cornice in the living room suggested new related trim around doorways whose heights were increased to nine feet. New ebonized ash doors were given black nickel knobs. Also added to purify the backgrounds was a sober, custom-designed limestone mantel paired with the plainest seventeenth-century andirons. Above the mantel was a scalloped mirror hand-carved from an original design by Jean-Michel Frank and finished in white gold. The walls were stippled and glazed a light stone color, the moldings painted soft ivory.

The console's lyre-shaped legs and, in the library, the bird's-eye maple stools on "X" supports, all honor Mr. Frank.

SOUTHERN COMFORT *(left)*

A. Herbert Rodgers, to whom Albert Hadley was apprenticed early in his career, was the architect of the neo-Georgian house in Nashville that includes this drawing room, and which Mr. Hadley recently advised on. Built in 1931, Brook House is today filled with the finest George III furniture, including the cabinet between the tall, elaborately curtained windows; French furniture from the same period; the finest contemporary upholstery; and works by Renoir, Bonnard, Boudin, and Homer.

TWIN PASSIONS *(following page)*

A bachelor's twin passions — furnishings of the Art Deco period and entertaining his wide circle of friends — shaped the decoration of his penthouse duplex. With Elizabeth Hammond as architect, two rather banal apartments were fashioned into a single luxurious unit comprised of the principal public and private rooms on the first floor and an extravagant conservatory on the second.

HOLDING BACK FOR ARCHITECTURE *(above)*

The "hands-off" decoration of Mr. and Mrs. Leonard Newman's double-height living room cedes to Romaldo Giurgola's monumental architecture. "Hands-off" means down-filled seating and a palette of pales for the canvas covers, cotton-and-jute rug, and plaster walls. In a room that is all about control, the limestone chimneypiece is French, the lacquer table Oriental.

HIGH STYLE IN THE HILLS ABOVE SAN FRANCISCO *(right)*

A high-ceilinged penthouse is a vitrine of museum-quality objects and paintings, including a large Italian floral study, representing four centuries of European art. Below a rock crystal Genoese chandelier, modern upholstery is perfectly at home with Fortuny-covered gilt open-arm chairs.

MANHATTAN TRANSFER

In 1982 Albert Hadley undertook the redesign of the landmark Nelson Rockefeller apartment on Fifth Avenue. Many of the rooms had first been done in 1937 by the reductive modernist Jean-Michel Frank, working jointly on furnishings with Christian Bérard and Diego and Alberto Giacometti. After her husband's death, Mrs. Rockefeller sold off part of the apartment, including what had been the living room, and made plans to live on a more practical scale and in a less public way with her two sons. Albert Hadley advised her that she had a responsibility to preserve the atmosphere of rooms representing a turning point in twentieth-century decorative arts.

In the entrance hall, an Aubusson floral carpet in the neo-Romantic style by Christian Bérard is laid over wood flooring. Opposite an Edo-period Japanese screen and beside the Lehmbruck figure, a Frank side chair is covered in a clear shade of blue silk. Gilded bronze appliques in the form of hand-held goblets, so surreal and baroque, are by Alberto Giacometti. The original living room was much larger, yet almost all of its custom-designed furnishings were accommodated in the new space. These included, by Frank, armchairs with lithe giltwood frames and lean side tables entirely veneered in ivory. Diego and Alberto Giacometti contributed lamps, firedogs, and consoles. Flanking the fireplace below small works by Klee, the powerful robust consoles have vertical members evoking winged serpents. Fernand Léger's biomorphic free-form cove ceiling is fitted with cathode gas-tube lighting.

BETTER WITH TIME *(above and right)*

"My big triumph is having saved it from fresh paint — not a lick since 1969," Albert Hadley says of this pale gray New Jersey salon, whose pilasters and dental cornice were salvaged from a neighboring historic building.

Classic upholstered furniture, Hepplewhite chairs, and Regency benches form three seating groups on perfectly bare parquet. Fabrics are kept to chintz, silk, and ivory cotton. As for lighting, opaline glass, wooden urns, and tole columns are a nice break from Chinese porcelain.

GO FOR IT *(preceding page)*

Lustrous peacock-colored walls and a floor stained hot fudge and biscuit in alternating bands two, three, and four planks wide were the jazzy, high-octane backgrounds in a mid-1970s Manhattan living room. Parish-Hadley in collaboration with Alan Campbell created a handful of eye-bending custom-designed batik fabrics used for the sofa pillows. Chrome, glass, Lucite, fur, black lacquer, crunchy white damask, animal spots, and voluptuous brown satin were all stirred together. Over the sofa, as a foil to all the pulsing pattern, a Larry Poons.

LIVING IN A SINGLE ROOM

Home to Glenn Bernbaum, proprietor of Mortimer's
on the Upper East Side, is his restaurant's former
kitchen and supply room. Blasting them away to
create a single space of eleven hundred square feet,
he spent a year getting rid of an air shaft, only to
have Albert Hadley announce that he planned to
add a freestanding column that would enclose the
refrigerator and that everyone would think was
structural. His one, mostly beige loftlike room is di-
vided into areas for sleeping, dining and cooking,
and "living."

MODERN CLASSICS *(following page)*

Parish-Hadley's collection for Baker Furniture is
based on thirties, forties, and neoclassical designs.
The result: modern classics with the chameleon ability to integrate themselves in almost any scheme.
Wood bases give the sofas a sharp silhouette, and
gold leaf, black lacquer, and faux tortoise are among
the wealthy finishes.

71

＊

Dining Rooms

THE DINING ROOM, Town . . . taffeta balloon shades, an heirloom Bessarabian . . . & Country . . . natural muslin curtains, wide pegged floorboards the color of plum pudding . . .

＊

the mismatched appeal of a decoupage tabletop dancing with blackamoors set on a gilt-iron base . . .

＊

collections on display . . . playful ceramic fruits and vegetables, dozens of trophies, armfuls of blue-and-white china . . .

＊

the unexpected comfort of a loose downy pillow thrown into a dining chair . . .

＊

doubling up: the dining room as library, as sitting room . . .

＊

an effective shield against kitchen noise and light: a service door that swings out . . .

＊

the good sense of a separate breakfast table . . .

＊

centerpieces with power: a Thai woven lacquer box, a fanciful papier-mâché gourd . . .

＊

the bare minimum: one candle for every two people at table; mixing it up for sexy shadows: high light and low light; low-voltage strip-lighting in corners, under tables . . .

NEVER LETTING GO *(preceding page)*

The gay romantic trompe l'oeil wall canvases, Directoire painted chairs, and gold-lit Louis XVI corner console in Mrs. Parish's old dining room at 39 East 79th Street started out in her parents' Paris pied-à-terre at 23 quai d'Orsay. The Italian canvases were part of what originally started her thinking, during a trip to France at age eighteen in 1928, about beauty and the way things look. She was not about to let them go after discovering them rolled up in the family attic in New Jersey.

The decorative covered dish instead of a floral certerpiece — in this case a Chelsea melon found by her mother in Rome — is typical of Mrs. Parish. Below a Russian chandelier that hangs today in the entrance hall of her maisonette and that mixes crystal with emerald and ruby glass, the eighteenth-century French mahogany table is set with family silver and Battersea candlesticks.

INSPIRED BY ROMANCE *(above)*

The scheme for the dining room was built around a garlanded series of pastoral paper panels by Jean Pillement, who in 1778 was appointed painter to Marie Antoinette and who contributed three works to the Petit Trianon. Above the dado, the walls were painted a deep rich peacock blue to throw the murals into high relief.

Tall French windows giving onto a small terrace were fancifully curtained in haute ball-gown fashion in silk taffeta. Louis XV armchairs with loose apple-green seat pads were matched to a French eighteenth-century mahogany dining table set with silver chargers, single blossoms at each setting, Bohemian glass, and metal centerpieces composed of palm trees and camels bought in a Cairo bazaar and later silvered.

A MULTI-USE DINING ROOM

Using the English-country-house technique of glazing with a whisk broom, Albert Hadley created animated backgrounds in a Manhattan dining room furnished with a curvilinear sofa. Bookcases carry through the idea of a multi-use space.

Hurricane globes with smoke bells mounted as sconces were electrified using tiny, clear, flame-shaped bulbs. Curtains are in festooned and fringed glazed chintz, and Victorian chairs frame a serpentine sideboard.

ALBERT HADLEY: "FORT WILLIAM" *(left)*

The Tarrytown, New York, farmhouse that includes this dining room–library was built in 1851. Albert Hadley, whose country retreat it was for many years, referred to it as "a scrapbook."

To create an access to the adjacent porch, a double-hung window was replaced by a door that maintained the design of the original opening. Centering the room was a claw-foot mahogany pedestal table surrounded by whitewashed armchairs.

ROOMS OF ONE'S OWN *(above)*

When Bunny Williams first met Mrs. Peter Logan, she was living — not too happily, Mrs. Williams thought — in Weston, Massachusetts, in a modern house surrounded by modern things. The purpose of the meeting was to begin organizing Mrs. Logan's move from Weston to a nineteenth-century farmhouse on the Maine coast. But before anything could be done, Mrs. Williams said, she had to find out why the Massachusetts house and her new client had been so mismatched. The answer was in dozens of manila envelopes Mrs. Logan had privately filled with magazine clippings. What she liked about them, even if she was unable to articulate it, was how strongly they communicated the enthusiasms, personal style, and eccentricities of their owners. Mrs. Logan revealed herself to be a lover of books, mudrooms, wicker, needlepoint, music, American Indian crafts, earthenware, and everything to do with the botanical world.

Planted on a low cliff 150 feet from the sea in the town of Ogunquit, the house incorporates a tavern that was transported from nearby York in 1932. All of the pine paneling and wide-planked floors are original to the house, while freestanding carpenter-made bookcases of a plain custom design in the same wood were added in the library and dining room. To house a collection of important botanical works, a tiny library was fashioned out of the original borning room.

THE EUROPEANS

Except for the all-too-familiar window placement that gives this dining room away as being in New York, one would be challenged to guess that one was not in Europe. The suitability of the grand setting is in any case unquestioned because the owners of the apartment were born abroad into families for whom this sort of luxe decoration was natural and assumed. The young parents of two small boys, both have a keen knowledge of art and decoration. For Parish-Hadley, working with highly sophisticated people with highly sophisticated taste made the project an enormous pleasure and challenge, which was to create a background equal to the quality and ornamental nature of the furnishings and objects. The simplest and most direct way of effecting this was to use the same silk in a wide self-stripe to upholster walls, for the softly draped curtains at the double window, and for the small banquettes flanking the monogrammed door into the drawing room. While carefully editing an eclectic assemblage of rather rarefied components, it was crucial to keep in mind that this is a contemporary room for vital people, a room that functions largely as an everyday dining room for the family of four. In the end it was a case of great treasures casually deployed, though casual is not to be confused with reckless or sloppy. Casual here means civilized informality.

On the long wall opposite the entrance from the stair hall, a quite unbelievable *c.* 1740 giltwood console is positioned below *Still Life with Trumpet and Kettledrums* (1760) by Nicolas-Henry Jeurat de Bertry, a painter popular with the French royal family and Parisian aristocracy. It is thought that the work, representing a heavy cavalry regiment's honor pieces, was commissioned by the wife of Louis XV as a gift to a favorite regiment. Opposite the console and of similar size, a table is casually draped with a striking Flemish tapestry that sweeps the floor. Surprisingly enough, the early-twentieth-century abstract rug is French.

Adequate for small dinners, the 1837 Johnson & Jupe table that centers the room is surrounded by eighteenth-century painted Genovese chairs, adding an element of playfulness to a scheme that could very easily have become overwrought with grandeur. For large parties, buffets are set and small tables placed around the apartment. On such occasions the banquettes become the focal points for intimate groups of four or six. One of the most original touches in this jewellike environment are the Charmian Stirling studies of one of the owners' sons in an elaborately carved giltwood frame before the window.

A NEW YORK FANTASY *(left)*

The light, heady, almost giddy decoration of this small and square New York dining room was inspired by the interiors at Liselund in Denmark, built in 1792. Console tables with marbleized tops display mercury glass lamps with finely pleated silk shades wittily edged in glass ball fringe.

THE DINING ROOM AS PRINT ROOM *(above)*

In a Florida dining room, eighty monochrome chinoiserie plaques in simplified rococo shapes were inspired by a paper in the Chinese bedroom at Carton near Dublin and painted by Chuck Fischer. Against the chartreuse glazed wall is a mid-nineteenth-century English console with cabriole legs; mahogany chairs in the Chippendale style are from the same period.

FRAMING THE VIEW *(following page)*

In a New York dining room, squares of Chinese silver tea paper create a cool and glamorous backdrop for a collection of sharp twentieth-century furnishings, including Carl Witzman ebonized chairs and a table composed of a bronze base and granite top banded in the same metal.

Libraries

THE LIBRARY as escape, as private domain (knock before entering) . . .

on the other hand, the library as dining room–cum–art gallery . . .

a generous book table covered in plainest felt . . .

book bindings rich enough to supply the decoration . . .

morocco-bound first editions in exotic wood cases behind brass grilles . . .

the usefulness of a currently accurate, easy-to-read globe . . .

Rameau (or rock or rap) before the fire . . .

portfolios in a stand for consulting prints, documents . . .

a good, substantial — and safe — ladder . . .

the most comfortable seating in the house . . .

the learned appeal of floor-to-ceiling bookcases . . .

a boulle cabinet as drinks table . . .

a place for scholarship, trophies, personal memorabilia (your picture
with the president) . . .

MODEL LIBRARY

A ground-floor bedroom in a Georgian-style house was transformed into a library by architect Robert Raley and Parish-Hadley. For comfort and practicality, it was furnished with a Chippendale center table, Russian armchairs, and a seventeenth-century Chinese rug. The glass bookshelves have concealed strip lighting for subtle illumination. Niches above the mahogany doors display busts of George Washington and Benjamin Franklin. Brass grillwork doors protect without obscuring from view the fine collection of first editions assembled within.

HAIL BRITANNIA

Needlework pillows, linen upholstery, tray tables, swagged curtains, pine paneling, leather-lined bookcases, dog pictures — all evoke the civility special to country-house living in England. Except that here we are in a Park Avenue library, where placed beside an eighteenth-century bergère in tobacco silk is a Regency center table with a base of dolphins and cattails. The chairs around the custom-designed brass card table are also Regency.

BOOKS AS ART *(right)*

Enid Annenberg Haupt is known for her idiosyncratic display of oversized books, many on botanical subjects, as small works of art, casually leaning them against a wall, perhaps, or the leg of a commode. Used for studying, the table has a plain, utilitarian felt cloth.

ALBERT HADLEY'S SANG-DE-BOEUF LIBRARY FOR BROOKE ASTOR
(following page)

Brooke Astor's motivation for redoing her Park Avenue library was to devise a showcase for the three thousand volumes assembled by her late husband. Albert Hadley proposed recessed floor-to-ceiling shelves, sang-de-boeuf enamel for the walls, and brass trim. Since precision was crucial, the wooden wall panels were built directly in the apartment, then sent to the foundry for their metalwork. "Everything had to fit like jewelry," says Mr. Hadley. Reassembled in the library, they were treated to numerous coats of lacquerlike enamel, each rubbed with a fine pumice stone, followed by the application of a mottled glaze. Lastly, the walls were given a gloss varnish, then polished three times.

To keep all the red from spilling into the hall and drawing room, the doors and recesses between the library and those rooms were mirrored.

Bedrooms

THE BEDROOM as sanctuary . . .

*

the potential for fantasy — what dreams are made of . . .

*

every day: fresh linens, fresh garden flowers . . .

*

whether futon or four-poster, a bed that sets the tone . . .

*

within reach: a pharmacy lamp, a flashlight, a box of chocolates . . .

*

at the foot of the bed, a pop-up television in an antique trunk . . .

*

sleep masks and Elvis blackout shades . . .

*

a well-placed table for writing, dining . . .

*

"white-noise" sound machines for getting to sleep . . .

*

a guest room's private terrace, sun deck, garden . . .

*

a dog bed that's not a basket . . .

*

the bedroom as office, the bed as desk — as command central . . .

*

embracing the beauty of electronic controls in a bedside drawer . . .

*

getting up with the sun . . .

A PREFERENCE FOR FLOWERS *(preceding page)*

Reflected in an eighteenth-century trumeau, even the demi-lune night table in this Manhattan bedroom was pasted with lattice chintz to keep the room from looking as though it is crowded with furniture. Silk-embroidered religious figures from the same period are Venetian, and an old flaking wrought-iron planting table displays photographs.

THE PRINCESS MARGARET BEDROOM *(above and right)*

A visit by Princess Margaret and Lord Snowden to Greentree, the Long Island estate of Mr. and Mrs. John Hay Whitney, prompted the freshening of the entire guest wing, including, for the royal visitors, two bedrooms, a sitting room, and bath. To create a proper suite for the recently married couple in which the two bedrooms adjoined, a closet to the right of the fireplace was knocked through without disturbing the existing nineteenth-century French scenic paper. New natural linen roller shades edged with heavy Irish lace and tone-on-tone Swiss muslin curtains finished with loop fringe were hung below gently draped valances in the Empire style, caught up by brass rosettes set directly under the cornice. With its echoing drapery and Louis XVI fruitwood armchair, the dressing table held a triptych mirror and whimsical bronze candlestick lamps in the form of giraffes and palm trees. To remind the queen's sister that she was in America, the new bed with a cotton mate-lassé headboard was given a graphic patchwork quilt, and the floor was scattered with a number of small hooked rugs.

ANTEBELLUM GOODNIGHT *(above)*

A Florida guest room with views of Tampa Bay features a distinctive bed as the centerpiece. A nineteenth-century spool-turned bed from the American South anchors this guest room. An antique woven spread and handblocked fabric for the table cover reinforce the American theme.

PASSAGE TO INDIA *(right)*

This small Manhattan bedroom was created for a young executive who happened to have a very lively interest in decoration and the ancillary interest in color and comfort and luxury that goes with it. Concern for such things naturally resulted in his having certain fixed ideas about the kind of room he wanted and what would go in it. For example, the man knew he wanted an upholstered sleigh bed.

The eye-filling scheme combined Indian cottons of similar all-over pattern but different scale, the border of one delineating the form of the bed and edging the lightly stitched cover. The fabrics themselves are modern-day versions of the *indiènnes* that entered Marseilles from India in the seventeenth century and that had such great success at Versailles with the court of Louis XIV.

Blue was the accent color, subtly diffused by the needlework rug and Chinese porcelains on the table and in the painting, and more boldly by the cashmere throw and taffeta curtains hung from an exotic carved and painted pelmet fringed with gilded wooden coins and tassels. While many men might find the sophistication of the finished scheme a bit overwhelming for everyday life, this young executive did not.

GOING TO SLEEP IN A STRAWBERRY PATCH *(preceding page)*

In a Palm Beach guest house that faces the sea, juicy, leafy, oversized strawberries on a natural canvas ground smother the beds, walls, and windows while also covering the cushions of two beefy Lucite stools. The beds themselves are of black tole with head- and footboards in the form of star-studded medallions suspended in brackets. More red for the smart lacquer night table and cranberry glass lamp.

THE BEST GUEST ROOM *(above and left)*

The client's reminiscences of past visits to English country houses inspired the decoration of this principal, or best, guest room. Paisley-patterned carpet supplies ample pattern to anchor the impressive four-poster canopy bed. A pair of English japanned chests serve as nightstands, while a wheel-back Hepplewhite settee is silhouetted in front of French doors that open to reveal the fields and paddocks outside. Leading the way to this room is a hall balcony that overlooks the double-height library below.

THE RIGHT STUFFS *(preceding page)*

"Nothing was bought just to fill up the rooms," Albert Hadley says of Annette de la Renta's Federal-style house in Katonah, New York, which was built some sixty years ago. "Rather, everything was bought because it has a particular allure for Annette. In that sense, I would say the house is undecorated. When decorators try to do the same thing, it often amounts to nothing more than decoration because the rooms do not make a personal statement."

The statement in this bedroom is made with stuffs blazing with color, including a wealth of nineteenth-century chintzes and serges from England, France, and Portugal. Supplied by Elinor Merrell, the leading fabrics authority, they were stitched into bed hangings, for the American Empire mahogany four-poster, and used to cover furniture. Needlework — cushions, chair covers, and rugs of the same vintage — was also procured. The double bonnet-top secretary desk stands proudly between the windows holding a collection of Japanese teapots.

"In this more than any other room in the house, Annette's warmth, coziness, and sense of luxury come through," says Mr. Hadley. "And it reflects her love of England. Working with her is always exhilarating. She's not finicky-caring; she just wants to get it right. And sometimes she wants it a little wrong in order to make it right. The effect is more important to Annette than dry textbook scholarship."

REVERSE LUXURY *(right)*

In a New York townhouse, Parish-Hadley's own stylized moiré, based on an Early American document, was used for walls, curtains, and bed hangings. This background pattern pulled together the owner's rather diverse mix of period marquetry and ormulu-mounted lacquered furniture. In a kind of reverse statement about luxury, the nineteenth-century bed in the Louis XVI style displays its embroidered sheets and blanket cover. A bleached pine Art Deco screen heightens the hushed confidentiality underlying this alluring bedroom.

Garden Rooms

shelter from the storm . . .

＊

cashmere throws at nap time . . .

＊

public vs. private: the front porch vs. the back . . .

＊

a room with a view . . .

＊

shucking the corn harvest . . .

＊

high-summer midnight supper . . .

＊

wicker and straw, canvas and iron, sisal and screening,
bamboo and duck, rattan and hemp . . .

＊

chunky, hand-blown hurricane globes . . .

＊

the surprise of a mirror . . .

＊

just outside: a birdbath, an obelisk, the sea . . .

＊

never more appropriate: an Aiken sofa, treillage . . .

＊

the whir of ceiling fans . . .

＊

the smell of freshly mowed grass . . .

INSIDE OUT

A show-house garden room in a Greenwich, Connecticut, house once belonging to the Gimbel family was glazed a rich woodsy green and filled with ferns and ficus as a way of confusing the boundaries between inside and out. Light and fresh and happy, the room gamely tossed together toile de Jouy and glazed candy-striped cotton with a romantic English nineteenth-century painted leather screen, an Adirondack-style twig table, and an ornamental tole canister. An elaborate wood-and-iron chandelier hangs above this animated mixture.

OUTDOOR LIVING IN THE PACIFIC NORTHWEST *(left)*

Filled with antique wicker furniture, a lush all-green-and-white terrace outside Seattle is pitched steeply above a formal garden edged by wilderness. Below a canopy of grape vines, itself covered by a glass ceiling, canvas curtains have lattice trim echoing the panels of ironwork.

A SEASIDE GARDEN ROOM *(above)*

Trompe l'oeil bamboo latticework was designed to go hand-in-glove with deep-seated bamboo furniture, its cushions of hand-painted canvas, in a garden room for Mrs. Thomas Jefferson Coolidge in Manchester, Massachusetts. Bowing to the natural beauty of the setting — the house was on a headland surrounded on three sides by the Atlantic — architect Page Cross angled it to the ocean, rather than positioning it straight on, in order to capture a distant view of coves beyond sweeping lawns. A single bamboo roller shade controlled not only the light in the room but the circulation of air. An Italian lacquer lantern hung from a ceiling painted pale melon to pick up the pinkness of the natural brick floor, laid with a lacy Spanish straw rug.

CHOICE SOLARIUMS (preceding page)

One of two glass-enclosed garden rooms at opposite ends of a house situated on a sixty-eight-acre estate in New York's Westchester County, arranged for long hours of reading, private contemplation, and the spirited conversation of houseguests. Each is generously furnished with tailored upholstered seating; the rooms have cool floor tiles and present the option of thickly wooded views or of views of terraced gardens and the hills across the Hudson.

A HANGING BASKET GARDEN

(above and right)

With its crisp black screens popping out from white walls and a white enamel ceiling, this upstate New York porch has dining and sitting areas defined by matching sisal rugs hand-stenciled with lattice and Greek Key designs. A majolica garden seat and two custom wooden pole lamps with woven paper shades are posed on a floor that was treated to five shades of green before the final mottled effect was achieved. At the other end of the room, Elsie de Wolfe's famous glazed fern chintz turns up on a Windsor chair and a couple of spoon-backs.

✳

The Kennedy

White House

In 1961 Mrs. Parish made history with President and Mrs. John F. Kennedy by giving the First Family private living quarters in the White House that were practical and comfortable for the first time.

"Kennedys Add Kitchen, Pantry, Dining Room," trumpeted the *Louisville Courier-Journal*.

But Mrs. Parish did much more. Pre-Camelot, the State Rooms were decorated with broadloom carpeting and department-store reproduction furniture. Mrs. Parish was a linchpin of the Fine Arts Committee created to bring together, through donations, what would replace the geegaws: museum-quality furnishings tracing the history of the American presidency. Early members were enlisted at her suggestion. One of these, John L. Loeb, made it possible for his friend Sister Parish to entirely remake the Oval Room, the private yellow drawing room where the president also liked to receive heads of state.

Mrs. Parish even employed trompe l'oeil at the White House, relieving the dreariness of a couple of dark, heavy mantelpieces. Fascinated that she had marbleized marble, the public ran its feet across the hearths until they were worn back to real stone.

Between the election and the inauguration, Mrs. Parish's schemes for the Executive Mansion were done from tiny blueprints uncovered at the New York Public Library and based on consultations with Mrs. Kennedy.

Mrs. Parish shared her early White House impressions with C. David Heymann in *A Woman Named Jackie*, describing how she . . .

walked from room to room, opening closet doors and peeking into dark corners. . . . There was . . . much that would have to be discarded. . . .

The private living quarters were in terrible shape—spots on the carpets, falling plaster. . . . The greater problem had to do with the formal public rooms . . . [which] contained a hodge-podge of tables and chairs. The furniture lacked historical relevance. . . .

I told Mrs. Kennedy that to do the White House justice, it would have to be restored from top to bottom.

Mrs. Parish convinced her that she should have an upstairs family unit. Previous First Families had to go downstairs to the public areas in order to dine.

During their first week on the job, Mrs. Parish and Mrs. Kennedy also attacked the office of the president, who told them that his rocking chair must stay. Mrs. Kennedy winked at Mrs. Parish, whispering, "We'll get it out somehow." But it stayed.

Jayne Wrightsman was the shop hound for the Oval Room. Since this was a private room, Mrs. Kennedy could indulge her love of Louis XVI furniture.

"I found a set of furniture stamped J. LeLarge consisting of a canape and six side chairs," Mrs. Wrightsman wrote Mrs. Parish from Paris. "The model is completely charming and would completely furnish the [Oval] room."

Mrs. Kennedy worked on the curtains, writing to Mrs. Parish, "Here is Oval Room sketch — 2 shades of yellow taffeta — Undercurtains should be paler yellow. . . ."

Much of the furniture in the President's Dining Room, which was conceived as a showcase for the American Federal style, was made by eighteenth-century Maryland craftsmen. A sideboard with satinwood inlay in the form of an American eagle displayed silver purchased by Andrew Jackson. Curtains were based on a nineteenth-century documentary design.

I had known Mrs. Kennedy and worked with her during the 1960
Presidential Campaign on the Senator's house on N Street in
Washington and on their Cape Cod house.

After the election Mrs. Kennedy called me in New York and left
a message with my secretary, as I was out of town, asking me to
help her with "the house with the columns" as she phrased it.

THE WHITE HOUSE
WASHINGTON

Mrs. John F. Kennedy
The White House
Washington, D.C.

August 6, 1963

JOHN'S ROOM

18 yds blue and white printed cotton @ 5 25   94 50

MISCELLANEOUS

Six wastebaskets   33 00
Three pencil baskets   @ 5 50
Parcel Post   90   2 70
                                                     ─────
                                                      3 05
                                                    133 25

United States Senate
─────
MEMORANDUM

United States Senate
─────
MEMORANDUM

Domestic Staff at White House
Pledges Secrecy on Life There

White House
Will Undergo
Little Change

Mrs. Kennedy
Calls Decorator,
3 Art Experts

Design for V

The Washington Post
for and about WOMEN

WOMEN'S
CLASSIFIED
COMICS

SECTION D   FRIDAY, MARCH 3, 1961

In White House Remodeling

President Gets Kitchen Close By
For Midnight Refrigerator Raids

By Frances Lewine

POUR LE SALON OVALE

Une cheminée en marbre blanc et vert
ancienne Louis XVI.

Soit 1.42

Remise aux mesures de cette cheminée
pour adaptation dans la pièce.

Soit 910.-

Valeur Loco-magasin

Non compris : Emballage
               Transport
               Assurance

THE WHITE HOUSE
WASHINGTON

THE WHITE HOUSE
WASHINGTON

First Interview With Mrs. P

Decorator refuses to discuss
White House affiliations

MRS. HENRY PARISH II, INC.
22 EAST 69TH STREET
NEW YORK 21, N. Y.

THE WHITE HOUSE
WASHINGTON

THE WHITE HOUSE
WASHINGTON

August 25, 1961

Dear Mrs. Parish:

    Mrs. Kennedy thought you might like
to have a copy of the bill establishing the
White House as a national monument, which was
introduced by Senator Clinton Anderson on
August 15. A companion bill was recently introduced in the House of Representatives by
Congressman J. T. Rutherford.

    A copy of S.2422 is enclosed.

                            Sincerely,

                            Janet G. Felton
                            Secretary to
                            Fine Arts Committee

Mrs. Henry Parish, II
22 East 69th Street
New York City, New York

Mrs. Henry Parish II, Inc.
22 East 69th Street
New York 21, New York

Dearest Sister:

Thanks so much for your long letter about Gl

First Family Won't Make
Drastic Changes In Decor

By GAY PAULEY

87TH CONGRESS
1ST SESSION

S. 2422

IN THE SENATE OF THE UNIT

AUGUST 15, 1961

Mr. ANDERSON introduced the following bill; which w
to the Committee on Interior and Ins

A BILL

To establish the White House as a nat

1   Be it enacted by the Senate and
2 tives of the United States of America i
3 That all of that portion of reservation
4 city of Washington, District of Colum
5 the President's park enclosure, comp
6 seven one-hundredths acres, is hereby
7 tional monument to be known as the
8 shall be administered pursuant to the
9 1961 (39 Stat. 535; 16 U.S.C. 1-3), and
10 mentary thereto and amendatory thereof: Pr
11 such designation and administration shall emph

Forward, please !

Mrs. Helen Parish
Interior Decorator from New York City
Glen Ora

HOME FURNISHINGS DAILY
WEDNESDAY, JANUARY 25, 1961

John L. Loeb

July 7, 1961

THE WHITE HOUSE

Dear Mr. and Mrs. Loeb -

You cannot imagine how touched and appreciative I am that you want to help with our Oval Room - It is not a public room - so that makes you both so much more patriotic - to wish to help in a room which the thousands of tourists do not see (but they will in photographs).

It is my favorite room in The White House - the one where I think the heart of the White House is - where the President receives all the heads of state who visit him - where the honor guard if formed to march downstairs to "Hail to the Chief" - All the ceremony and all the private talks that really matter happen in that room - and it has the most beautiful proportions of any in the W. House.

It has always been so ghastly and so neglected - Every future President would be so happy to have it as a room he could be proud of - These are my thoughts on it - and you both must come and see it - and

TELEPHONE
RHInelander 4-5380

MRS. HENRY PARISH II. INC.
22 EAST 69th STREET
NEW YORK 21. N.Y.

Dear Mrs. Kennedy:

We have sifted through all your ...
... Mrs. Parsons has agreed to the ...
... and he have contacted Mr. Lloyd (who ...
... is to make an estimate for painting and wall ...
we will pass on to you. Miss Brophy is to ...
things which are going to country, on January ...
on January 19th. ... which china is to ...
everything goes smoothly.

We will take in room by room - ...

LIVING ROOM. It will take 33 yards of ...
for chairs, and 3 large pillows ...
will have something else (samples ...
New beige rug - waiting for your ...

DINING ROOM. (Walls green)
Suggest a dark rug, brown with flo...
and samples for curtains C ...

LIBRARY. As is

MRS. HENRY PARISH
22 EAST 69th STRE
NEW YORK 21, N.

Dear Jackie,

I received your latest picture ...
curtains. I am a little concerned a...
many changes. From the very start t...
the fringe and the galoon. It has ...
but it is ready. Mr. du Pont had a ...
drawing (enclosed also) to be hung ...
windows. The only change we were ...
the center window swag. A drawing ...
du Pont also approved of that. I ha...
of the galoon and of the fringe. Th...
the fringe is to have the heading w...
making the stars identical to your ...

The over curtain material is c...
heavy faille which you sent to us t...
curtain material we can change to th...
as they have only made the strike offs of the thr...
which you have for approval. (one in yellow, two ...

If you insist, this complete new treatment p...
drastic problem as the changes would require yard...
be totally different, plus the elimination of the ...
and an additional yardage of fringe.

I feel the original drawing is more appropri...
the room and the furniture. I agree that it ...
prettier if the over curtains were tied back.

We have alerted the work room, ...
that no further work should be done ...

FINE ARTS COMMITTEE FOR THE WHITE HOUSE
CHAIRMAN - MR. HENRY F. DU PONT
HONORARY CHAIRMAN - MRS. JOHN F. KENNEDY

THE WHITE HOUSE
WASHINGTON
September 19, 1961

Dear Sister:

These are the materials I have chosen on ...

President's Dining Room

Valance and jabots B&F #5168, blue taf...
Under curtains B&F #5167, lighter ...

Enclosed is a rough sketch.

Oval Room

1. Louis XVI canape and six fauteuils;

The pattern damask I sent to Mr. Kel...
which should be dyed the mustard yel...
Velvet #3695-25;

2. Tufted sofa, heavy poison green;
Thaibok TS 120-M (Supposedly will b...

3. The two Bergeres in same color Thaib...
textured, TS 141-A (In stock)

4. Fire Bench and four side chairs - S...

5. Curtains

I want to have contrasting colors in yellow, ...
is what I have decided (See sketch).

Oval Room curtains are to be heavy material y...
have just had made by Scalamandre with the br...
tured little balls made by him. (Please elim...
star braid and wide border braid.)

THE WHITE HOUSE
WASHINGTON
June 30, 1961

Dear Sister:

I understand so well that if John Loeb should
do the Oval Room he would like to do it with
you. In that case, of course, I would not use
the poison curtains which I have wanted all
winter and are exactly what I would like, but
we can find a perfectly wonderful one from
Mr. du Pont's curtain book - in fact he suggested a design for the room long ago which
is similar to what I have in mind.

So if John Loeb makes up his mind, the Oval
Room will be you and him. I will, of course,
never push him or ask you to, but if I don't
hear from him by July fifteenth, I must go
ahead and order the yellow curtains as planned.
I will get someone to pay for them and just
furnish the room piece meal. I am sure you
will agree we cannot stay out next winter with
floppy nylon glass curtains. We have had our
period of grace this year as people knew we
were moving in, but that room must have curtains and covered furniture by next fall. It
would be so lovely if you could do it - I just
hope things work out. If I should have to go
ahead, you will understand it is because the
President wishes to use the room as his formal
drawing room and I cannot wait any longer to
have it ready by fall.

Two gigantic things I must thank you for -
Guertler's painting the State Dining Room which
will make all the difference in the world and
the silk hangings and curtains for the Red Room.

THE WHITE HOUSE
WASHINGTON

Dear Sister -

HYANNIS PORT
MASSACHUSETTS

P.S. Could you also send me a lampshade
it shall be 11½ across. ...
(the present paper one is -) for a glass column
...lamp

Dear Mrs. Kennedy and Member...
of the Fine Arts Commi...
for the White House,

President Thomas Jefferson was ...
furnishing it fully for the firs...
... of the White House of the Treasury.
Mrs. Douglas Dillon of Washington, wife of the Secretary.

ANTIQUES SOUGHT
FOR WHITE HOUSE

Continued From Page 1, Col. 1

President's Wife Starts
Revamping Quarters

WASHINGTON—Mrs. Jacque-
line Kennedy began her first full
week in the White House by starting to redecorate the President's
family's living quarters.

Mrs. Henry Parish, II
22 East 69th Street
New York

Dearest Sister:

Could you tell me how much the littl...
Italian cupboard you got me for my ...
Dining Room cost? It came from Char...
think.

Thanks so much.

Love,

The
First Lady
SHE TELLS
HER PLANS
FOR THE
WHITE
HOUSE

LIFE

SEPTEMBER 1 · 1961 · 20¢

Rockers Are Back, Too

President's chair
launched trend

Chicago, Ill.—The rocking
chair is present in unprece-
dented numbers and variety in
furniture showrooms at the
American Furniture Mart and
the Merchandise Mart, where
the semi-annual home furnishings market is now under way.

Furniture buyers will view
and personally test rocking
chairs designed for the office,
patio, kitchen, television room
and bedroom. It's all a reac-
tion to the trend started when
President Kennedy was photo-
graphed in his office rocker.

...with great interest Mrs. Engelhard's
... of our meeting on Tuesday, February 21,
... the memorandum in which Mrs. Kennedy and
... listed the items most necessary for the

...lly in accord with Nos. III and IV of
... a report, Mr. Clifford's statement that
...tely deductible for tax purposes, and
... to be followed when a gift is offered
...wever, it seems to me there should be a
... end for all members of the Committee to
... use when asking for gifts. Also, it would save much
time and effort if printed in this letter would be a
list of what is needed for the Green, Blue and Red
Rooms, the State Dining Room, and the Downstairs Family
Dining Room, as per memorandum; also in the East Room.

Inaugural Committee
Washington 25, D.C.

MADISON AVENUE
NEW YORK

...ry Parish, II,
...69th Street,
...N.Y.

XVI gilt bronze gueridons
XVI gilt bronze bouillotte
...mahogany table with rounded
...re fauteuil de bureau
...ther signed: Jacob

...for the lot

NO tax - for Resale.

Mr. and Mrs. Henry Parish IV
22 East 69th Street
New York
N.Y.

REGISTERED
488962
DO NOT BEND

Opposite top: The yellow drawing room as seen from the entrance into the room.

Opposite bottom: Eighteenth-century French furniture combined with luxurious contemporary upholstery made this an inviting room for President Kennedy and his family as well as heads of state.

Above: The president's new upstairs private dining room.

Overleaf: Scheme boards presented to President and Mrs. Kennedy for the family quarters.

Page 130, top: The second floor central hall comfortably furnished as the family living room.

Page 130, bottom: A very pretty and cheerful scheme was chosen for young Caroline's room.

Page 131, top: Mrs. Kennedy's bedroom featured a contemporary silk-screened cotton fabric.

Page 131, bottom: Mrs. Kennedy's personal collection of drawings, objects, and some French furniture animated the room.

OVAL ROOM

THE BLUE ROOM

EAST & WEST WINGS

FOR THE WHITE HOUSE: OVAL ROOM

Two "Jacob" Bergeres recovered in apricot moire, finished with guimp			
7 yards of moire required		12 75	89 25
1 yard plain taffeta for outside backs			19 50
20 yards of apricot and cream guimp @	3 00		60 00
10 yards of corded guimp		3 00	30 00
Labor charge	Each	145 00	290 00
Six Louis XVI Arm chairs; Four Side chairs; One Canape - all recovered in mustard gold cut velvet, finished with guimp			
40 yards of velvet required @	37 50		1500 00
85 yards of corded guimp @	6 75		573 75
64 yards of corded welt @	3 75		240 00
Labor charge 6 arm chairs @	110 00		660 00
4 side chairs @	100 00		400 00
1 canape			260 00
Charge to unpack cases in which above furniture was crated, and cartage to upholsterer, as well as candelabra and a pair of firedogs			103 75
One "Jacob" Bench recovered in green silk texture, finished with guimp			
1 yard required			34 50
3 yards of special guimp and 3 yards of cord welt			87 50
Labor charge			48 00
To wire Louis XVI Bronze dore and rock crystal chandelier with 6" wax candles, concealing the wires on the arms by cementing and matching the wires to the arms; provide special chain and ceiling plate. Deliver, assemble and install the chandelier in the Oval Room			2145 00

Three new pairs curtains			
Labor @ 185.00		555 00	
98 yards taffeta @ 12.75		1249 50	1,804 50
			$6,903 28

Curtains of Ivory Taffeta, edged with
...l loop fringe
...g with border in 3 shades of gold
...ront lined with Saffron Faille, tacked
... guimp

Curtains for the Family Dining
THE WHITE HOUSE

PRESIDENT'S
STUDY

22'

25x38'

20'x22'

THE FAMILY

BATH

President's Bedroom

UNDERCURTAINS
~~#1001~~

Mrs Kennedy's Bedroom

Valance 1001
Glazed Curtains

Two pair White Ta...
draw under Printe...
flat, shaped val...

Bench and Chair c...

BATHR...
White Tambour cur...
cotton carpet

Dining Room

Back Border

TRIM SCALE FL370-CF02

BREAKFRONT TRIM SCALE 55V157

Baby & Nurse's Room

UNDERCURTAINS CAREER 30771

LINCOLN ROOM 223 | MONROE ROOM 322

PRESIDENT'S STUDY 221 | PRESIDENT'S BED ROOM 220 | FIRST LADY'S BED ROOM 219 | FIRST LADY'S SITTING ROOM 218

CLOS. | CLOS.

BATH ROOM | PASSAGE | CLOS. | BATH ROOM

CENTER HALL | WEST SITTING HALL 229

Books | Books | Books

BATH ROOM | CLOS | NORTH HALL | CLOS | BATH ROOM | ELEV. | ELEV. VEST. | CLOS | CLOS | ELEV

MISS CAROLINE'S ROOM

White wool rug

Curtains of Rosebud Chintz, shirred valances
   piped with pink; Undercurtains of
   rosebud organdy

White canopy bed draped in Rosebud chintz,
   pink linings

Small Sofa - Rosebud chintz

Armchair - small red and white print

Through the Years

More than any other American decorating firm, Parish-Hadley is distinguished by the mutually nourishing ongoing rapport it enjoys with its clients. "Ongoing" can literally mean decades-spanning. Typically, the decoration of a city apartment leads to the decoration of a weekend house not far from town, which in turn leads to the decoration of a southern winter retreat.

Neither it is unusual for Parish-Hadley to execute several projects for the same people at the same time. The opportunities to explore varied and exciting solutions to different situations based on location and use of houses have led to many rewarding collaborations. While multiple commissions for a single client is the subject of this chapter, the company has in many cases decorated more properties than are actually shown.

Even once a house is "done," that does not mean Parish-Hadley's job is finished. "Freshening" is the word Mrs. Parish uses to describe the kind of light work necessary after years of "wear and love." Often the work is barely perceptible. It could be the replacement of a pair of curtain headings, or the rehabilitation of the buttons on a stool. Often it is the result of children grown and moved away that leads to new functions and therefore new forms to old rooms. It is precisely this continuity with clients and projects executed over time that has amplified Parish-Hadley's philosophy of design and decoration.

FAR HILLS, NEW JERSEY

Mrs. Parish first decorated this formal drawing room in the 1940s. The client was her cousin. Eventually the estate passed to the woman's son and it became apparent that, in Albert Hadley's words, "some simplification and maintenance, clarification, and reordering" were needed. This meant brushing (not dry cleaning) the curtains, new slipcovers, and fresh lamp and window shades.

Referred to with affection by the son who inherited it as a "Victorian Jacobean white elephant," the house is reached through an avenue of poplars and built of local stone. Chestnut trees on the property supplied the paneling for many of the interiors, and it was Mrs. Parish's idea all those years ago to lighten it with oyster-colored paint. While the walls had only become more beautiful since acquiring a patina, mournful tapestries were retired to the attic, and some of the heavy silk satins were traded in for gay candy-striped cotton. To strike a careful balance between old and new in the drawing room, the sofa's slate blue damask and the upholstery on the oval-backed Louis XVI chairs were retained. The pinks and reds of the eighteenth-century Aubusson rug set the raspberry-soufflé color scheme. Curtains were never even contemplated for the wide bank of windows, flanked by Chippendale mirrors, because the views of the landscape are just too enticing.

Fifty years after adding the classical pediment in this New Jersey country library, Mrs. Parish passed clients who like to say "they live in the past" on to Albert Hadley. Throughout the Victorian pile his job had more to do with what he calls "housekeeping" than with decorating.

The goal of a room that satisfies and entertains all the senses, that not only looks good but feels good, was attained by plundering the attic. Scraps of old velvet and antique paisley shawls were discovered and put to use as covering for cushions and stools. Trophies were repaired and polished and returned to their freshly waxed display cases. The original curtain bags, in a quality of linen no longer available, were remade into loose-fitting slipcovers by the housekeeper.

SUTTON PLACE, NEW YORK CITY

By editing and rearranging a trove of inherited furnishings for the same clients, a very contemporary view of luxury was expressed in their Manhattan apartment. In the entrance hall, Oriental rugs are used to delineate space, and a Louis XVI pouf is pulled up to a lacquer secretary.

The task in the living room was to create a stage for the string quartets that occasionally perform there. A Coromandel screen, parquet de Versailles, and boiseries carved with trumeaux supplied the backgrounds. Bringing the room into the late twentieth century are contemporary upholstered seating, striped silks, and plain taffeta curtains. A pouf balances the legginess of the chairs; indirect lighting suggests candlelight.

FIFTH AVENUE, NEW YORK CITY

The entrance hall of the Paleys' duplex was a long rectangular space that had been organized into three bays with bookcases and antique Italian parquet by Stéphane Boudin. Under Parish-Hadley, the walls and cases were painted cream to showcase the mellow old morocco bindings in olive, tan, and claret. Facsimiles of Oriental lacquer tables helped establish a warm library atmosphere.

Guests stepped off the elevator into a small vestibule that gave them the glamorous feeling they were standing inside a glass box. Squares of German glass, as thin as potato chips and with irregular waves, were held in place by gilded rosettes on walls glazed the color of deep bourbon.

The paneling in the salon was based on that in
the Hôtel Carnavalet in Paris. But rather than attempt a period re-creation, it was painted five different shades of high-gloss yellow, one each for the
undercoat, stiles, moldings, fields, and their cham-
fered edges. Placed at right angles to the center window, a boulle table broke the flow established by
three conversation groups, upholstered in earth-tone
Indian cottons and dull satins. A dyed goatskin rug
was sewn in twenty-four-inch squares.

MANHASSET, NEW YORK

William S. Paley and his stylish wife, whom almost everyone knew as Babe, were as interested in decorating as any two people in this century. Parish-Hadley did extensive work for the couple at Kiluna Farm, their late-nineteenth-century white clapboard house on Long Island. For the living room the Paleys wanted warmth, congeniality, and comfort. Its focus was an early-eighteenth-century French chimney-piece, which an ornamental Portuguese mirror served to relax. Louis XVI armchairs in linen velvet, and sofas in the same canvas as the walls, faced each other across an Oushak rug covering almost all of the green-painted floor.

SOUTHAMPTON, NEW YORK

Designed by Archibald Brown as a theater, Four Fountains was converted by the architect and his wife, Eleanor Brown of McMillen, in 1942. The couple made the auditorium, which measures forty by forty feet and has a twenty-foot ceiling, into a combined living room–dining room, walling off the stage and adding a double staircase to give access to the two bedrooms created there. While the inlaid lotus leaf–patterned floor in two shades of cork was retained, the projection room above the hall was taken over for two more bedrooms.

When the house was acquired by Mr. Paley, Parish-Hadley painted the big room soft apricot to suggest reflected firelight. The space boasted no less than seven seating groups — big, comfortable upholstered furniture stirred in with English and French chairs and tables made it perhaps the last word in all-in-one rooms. You could be alone or you could be fifty.

GREENWICH, CONNECTICUT

"It was a balancing act," says Alan Wanzenberg of Jed Johnson–Alan Wanzenberg Associates, the New York architect responsible for the conversion of this fieldstone barn designed in 1903 as a six-bay garage with chauffeur's quarters above. "I had to maintain the integrity of the original structure, which was extremely rich both in terms of style and craftsmanship, while also guaranteeing a lot of comfort for a man who is accustomed to it." Working in the English country-manor vernacular, Donn Barber, the original architect, employed fretwork balconies and masonry, hanging rafters, splayed rooflines, and deep eaves. The stone of the façade was quarried directly on the property.

Mr. Wanzenberg remembers that "on one of Mrs. Parish's first visits to the site we were walking around and she saw I had the cars parked in front of the east bay, visible from and on the same level as the living room. 'You've got it all wrong,' she said. 'You've got the cars driving around so far, and besides, it's obvious they should park on the west side where the turf drops down and they won't be seen.' She was right. She was always interested in prosaic questions like cars and service."

The original six-thousand-square-foot building had four good walls but no roof. Two wings totaling seven thousand square feet were added: one with servants' apartments, a garage, and a kitchen, and one with a master bedroom suite, a guest room, and a library with a double-height small-paned bay window. Mr. Wanzenberg says the project encouraged him to study an existing language of architecture and to employ that language in the house's remodeling and expansion. For example, since the garage's stone buttresses are repeated on the additions, it is difficult to tell where the old building ends and the new one begins.

Throughout the house the atmosphere is comfortable and relaxed despite the superb Sheraton, William Kent, and William and Mary furniture. While in the living room old rugs and bits of needlework were used to undercut the newness of glazed chintzes and cotton damasks, in the hall there is a Queen Anne Revival staircase, leafy 1874 William Morris "Larkspur" paper, nineteenth-century Karabagh rug, and antelope-spotted stair carpet.

LEXINGTON, KENTUCKY

The same client's historic horse farm in Lexington,
Kentucky, brought these words from Mrs. Parish the
first time she toured it: "The possibilities of this
house are regal." Queen Elizabeth, for her part, said
it could not have fallen into better hands than those
of the five-time Parish-Hadley client, who acquired
the bankrupt showplace at a court-ordered auction
for a well-publicized $17 million in 1992.

Set on 847 acres of sumptuous white-fenced pas-
tureland and with a mile-long drive leading to its
1939 columned clapboard manor house, Calumet
Farm was the mecca of thoroughbred breeding and
racing for sixty years, producing no less than nine
winners of the Kentucky Derby. Today, horses with
names like Conquistador Cielo and Danzig Connection fill the stables; Calumet is back in the running.

Having collaborated intimately with Mrs. Parish
on the client's other residences, David Kleinberg
was pleased to find that not only was the manor
house in excellent condition, it had been swept
clean. This "blank slate" made it easy for him to
imagine the look of "relaxed formality" he and Mrs.
Parish had agreed on.

Like much of the furniture, the English eighteenth-century mahogany chair in the entrance hall
was bought during a shopping trip to London.

MANHASSET, NEW YORK

When under Franklin Delano Roosevelt young members of the Whitney clan toured the White House, they found it nice but wanting. Nothing could compare, they said, with the family compound, Greentree, on Long Island.

Parish-Hadley's very personal involvement in the decoration of the shingled Colonial house for John Hay Whitney and Betsey Cushing Roosevelt Whitney (Mrs. Whitney had been married to the president's son James) dates to 1960. Today, collaborating perhaps more intimately with her than with any other client, the firm is charged with the general and never-finished task of what Mrs. Parish calls "freshening." Often this means fractionally improving what is already very good. It could be something as seemingly incidental as a new scarf to drape over the grand piano in the living room, whose outstanding feature is four-foot-high bookcases forming a strong horizontal band around the entire space, anchoring it. On the top shelf are rare orchids from the greenhouse, whimsical objects, and photographs. Flat velvet-pile carpeting is layered with colorful English needlework and primitive Mexican rugs.

BEEKMAN PLACE, NEW YORK CITY *(right)*

The furniture and objects in Mrs. Whitney's penthouse apartment were drawn from her former town house in the same neighborhood as well as from storerooms filled with family treasures. "It was done in a hurry, and carpets were one of the few items we had to shop for," says Mrs. Parish.

Paintings include a number of Cubist Picassos that first hung in Gertrude Stein's place in Paris. When Mrs. Parish and Mrs. Whitney meet, say, to discuss how the comfort of a twisted-rope stool might be heightened by removing four buttons from its upholstered seat, it is often in the living room of this apartment overlooking the East River.

SARATOGA, NEW YORK *(following page)*

In the late 1980s, Mrs. Whitney revived an 1880 clapboard horse farm in Saratoga that had belonged to her husband.

Working with Gary Hager, Mrs. Parish composed a sentimental, loudly sung hymn to Americana — an unpreachy sermon on the decorative wisdom of hooked rugs, needlework, quilts, and majolica. In a house committed to folk art with sporting and patriotic messages, the most popular motif is the American eagle, whether as a nineteenth-century New England weather vane or carved, embroidered, painted, or engraved. The farm is pure Mrs. Parish, right down to the early American flags and twig-and-rattan children's furniture deployed in grown-up rooms of great country sophistication.

Irregularly shaped, the entrance hall is dominated and centered by a large octagonal table, its richly layered coverings a playground for naif animated objects. High ceilings permitted a swagged paper border; without a second of agonizing or fuss, the border was cut down over the door where mouldings inconveniently were in the way.

A serious message couched in funny words, "no haute epoquery" was Mrs. Whitney's way of describing what she wanted left out.

WALDORF TOWERS, NEW YORK CITY

The living room of a suite on the fortieth floor of the Waldorf Towers was decorated for an industrialist and his wife in the late 1970s, drawing on the couple's museum-quality collection of French and other Continental furniture and objects. The walls were broken up with applied moldings and glazed a deep aubergine to frame panels of clear mirrored glass for a suitably traditional background that also injected the spark of drama. Even the rounded corners of the room were faced with mirror. Ormolu sconces, carved brackets holding Meissen birds, and Modigliani's *Doctor Spock* were hung directly against the reflective surfaces to heighten the illusion of distance and space, to create "instant" foregrounds and backgrounds.

A tall and dazzling Louis XVI drop-front desk separated the two seating groups. Against the windows, hung with flame-colored taffeta, was a low kidney-shaped sofa, all curves, made in Paris in the early 1950s. Cane and velvet, fruitwood and lacquer, old leather and old damask, marble and rock crystal, gave the room an opulent, many-layered feeling. But it was the mirror that made it.

LONDON, ENGLAND

An apartment in London's Grosvner House, as well as properties in various other locations — a seaside resort in Florida, a fishing compound in northern Canada, and the main family residence in New Jersey — was designed for the same couple at the same time as the Waldorf Suite.

Much of the furniture for this project had been transported from a former South African residence, the first project executed by Mrs. Parish for these clients, who have been friends since childhood. The glossiness of the primrose-yellow living room walls contrasted richly with the American cotton upholstery and curtain fabrics, most of which were created expressly for the apartment.

PARK AVENUE, NEW YORK CITY

A conventionally grand Park Avenue apartment first decorated by Mrs. Parish in the 1950s was gently nudged into the 1980s by Parish-Hadley for a client whose life had kept up with the times and whose collection of Géricaults, Tiepolos, and other Old Master drawings threatened to crowd her out. Undercutting the slightly Edwardian atmosphere of romance and femininity in the drawing room is a discipline and rigorousness that mirrors the owner's modern outlook.

In trying to undo some of the stateliness generic to a Manhattan apartment of the 1930s, an animated floral chintz was deployed in the principal reception room for elaborate swagged curtains with ruffled taffeta edges, on small Victorian chairs, and on Louis XV bergères and open-arm chairs. Well distributed throughout the room, the pattern was also chosen to play against and balance the silk moirés covering the sofas. For a less dressy effect, the period chairs were trimmed with plain flat ribbon in a contrasting color rather than with gimp or woven tape. Since the room is used constantly for entertaining, furniture was carefully organized in three groups to encourage fluid movement and easy conversation: except perhaps for the carved and gilded candy-striped tabourets, at a cocktail party for twenty, guests never find any reason to upset the seating. For intimacy, a low eight-panel Coromandel screen was placed behind the small buttoned sofa just inside the drawing room door, itself faced with panels of a Coromandel screen. Walls were stippled old ivory and the ceiling glazed a soft cloud pink.

Like the rest of the apartment, the owner found her bedroom too serious — she may have been getting older but her point of view was definitely getting younger. To lighten things up the Louis XVI bench and bergères were relieved of their sophisticated silks and satins and upholstered in multicolor tie-dye abstract cottons created especially for the room by Alan Campbell. A canopy bed from the same period was hung with creamy Swiss muslin caught up with cords and tassels, and a wool velvet broadloom rug was laid to soften the diamond-patterned painted floor. Beside the diagonally placed tub-back chaise longue, a delicate Regency faux bamboo chair was put with an early-nineteenth-century English mahogany kneehole desk. Inspired by the redecoration of her bedroom, with its tonic mix of tables in Lucite and glass and white lacquer, the owner bought the Richard Natkin painting centered above.

BRIARCLIFF, NEW YORK *(following page)*

The same client's Hudson River house has a long drawing room with a wide bay offering a view of terraced gardens and, beyond, rolling hills. The room's early-twentieth-century paneling was inspired by French boiseries of the mid eighteenth century, its recent paint finish reflecting the lightness associated with the earlier period. The sunny yellow of the silk taffeta curtains is repeated in various textures on some of the French chairs as well as on the soft luxurious pillows on four sofas anchoring as many seating groups.

In the generously proportioned dining room, a rich but subtle background was created by painting and glazing the walls in wide, alternating flat and lustrous stripes. The color: "elephant's breath." Softly shaped double-flounced valances top curtains of floral chintz, which is seen again on the four Louis XV–style armchairs.

CREDITS

PHOTO COORDINATOR: Ellen Horan

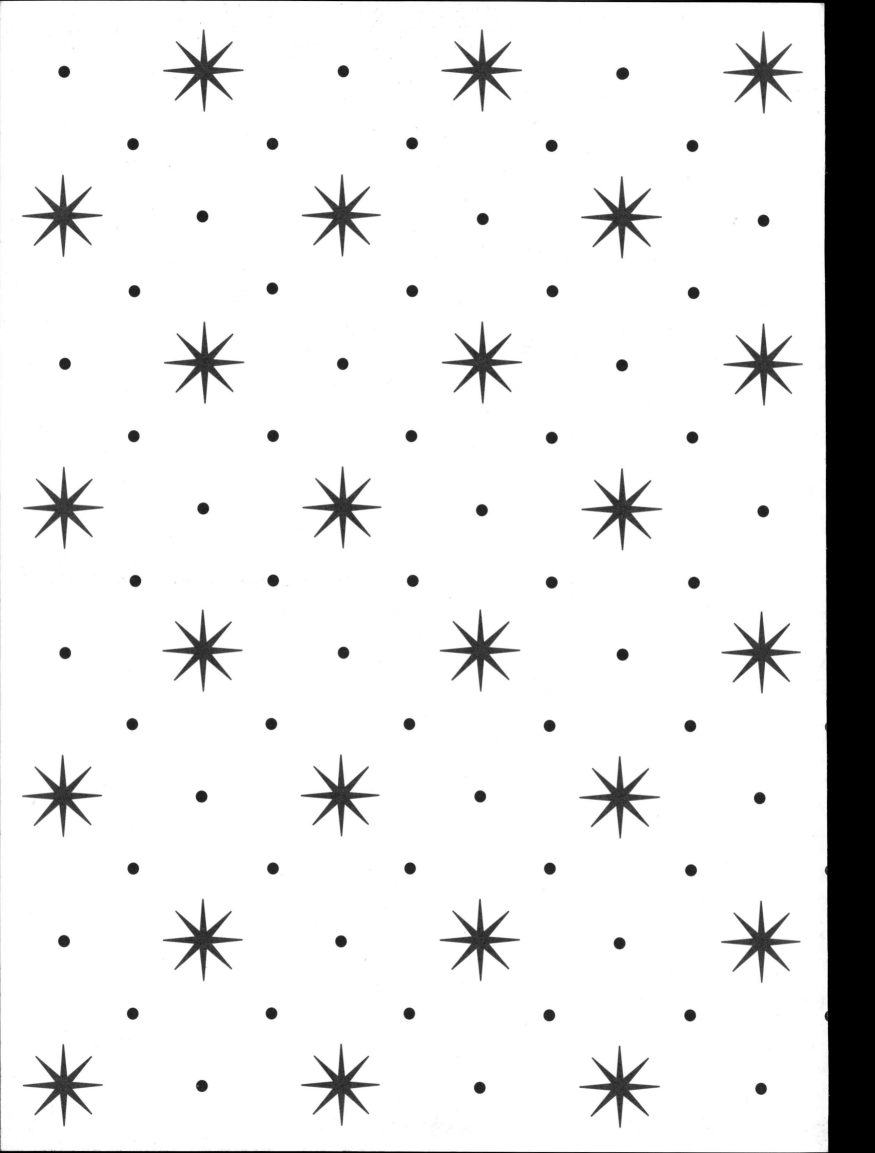